AF882602

The Injury Handbook

From Accident to Compensation

Insider Tips to Maximize your results

By

Christopher DiBella

Foreword by Charlie Moore, The Mad Fisherman

When life throws a curveball, as it often does, we find ourselves in searching for guidance. As a former client of Christopher DiBella and DiBella Law, I have navigated these waters personally and I am honored to write the foreword for this book.

For those who know me as the Mad Fisherman on TV, you're aware of my enthusiasm for life's adventures. Yet, when faced with needing an attorney, I found myself in a scenario no thrilling outdoor expedition could have prepared me for. It was during this time that I turned to the expertise of a remarkable attorney.

This book is more than just a guide, it's a lifeline for those entangled in the often perplexing world of personal injury law. Chris is a distinguished attorney with whom I've had the privilege of working with personally and is now someone I am proud to call a friend. Chris presents a wealth of knowledge in these pages. His personal experience being in an accident and knowing what his clients go through, shine through in every chapter, offering clarity and solace to those who find themselves on a similar path to the one he walked.

Whether you're grappling with the aftermath of an injury, standing at the crossroads of a legal battle, or simply seeking to understand the intricacies of personal injury law, this book is a must-read.

Chris's approach, combining professional insights with a deeply human touch, resonates with anyone looking for direction in turbulent times. His guidance is a testament to his unwavering commitment to advocating for those in need.

So, to anyone picking up this book, know that you hold a treasure trove of knowledge. It's a resource I wish I had been exposed to earlier on in my life and one I'm confident will aid you in your journey. As you turn each page, remember that you're not alone on this journey, thanks to Chris.

With gratitude and respect,

Charlie Moore The Mad Fisherman

Testimonials

1. "As someone who knew nothing about personal injury law, I found this book to be an invaluable resource. It's clear, concise, and made the legal process far less intimidating." – Paul L., Former Client
2. "Navigating a personal injury case was overwhelming, but this book became my go-to guide. The author's expertise and compassionate tone made a world of difference." – John C., Former Client
3. "From the emotional impact of a lawsuit to the nitty-gritty of legal proceedings, this book covers it all. It was like having a lawyer friend explain everything I needed to know." – Shannon W., Former Client
4. "The author's personal touch in explaining legal complexities was extremely moving. It's evident that this book is a labor of love and deep understanding." –Arthur B., Attorney
5. "This isn't your typical legal book, it's a heartfelt guide through the complexities of law and life. The personal anecdotes and compassionate advice are exactly what injured clients need." – Ken H. Attorney

Disclaimer

Please note that the information provided in this book is for educational and informational purposes only and is not intended as legal advice. The contents of this book are a general guide to understanding various aspects of the law and legal processes, particularly in the field of personal injury law. They should not be construed as specific legal advice for any individual case or situation.

The law varies significantly by jurisdiction, and the specific facts of your case can affect how the law applies to you. Therefore, it is crucial to consult with a qualified attorney in your area who can provide tailored legal advice based on the specifics of your case and the applicable laws in your jurisdiction.

This book does not establish an attorney-client relationship between the reader and the author or publisher. Any examples, scenarios, or hypothetical situations discussed in this book are illustrative and do not reflect actual cases.

Legal matters can be complex and nuanced, and seeking professional legal counsel is always advised for making informed decisions about your legal rights and options. We encourage readers to use the information in this book as a starting point for understanding legal concepts and to seek the guidance of an attorney for any legal issues or questions they may have.

Acknowledgment

First and foremost, I would like to express my deepest gratitude to my wife, my high school sweetheart, who has been my steadfast partner in life's journey. Her unwavering support and love have been my anchor through the challenges of law school and the demanding years of building my law firm. She has been a constant source of encouragement, wisdom, and strength, and for this, I am eternally grateful.

To my three wonderful children, my daughter and two sons, you bring immeasurable joy and purpose to my life. Your understanding, patience, and cheer have brightened my days and motivated me to strive for excellence, not only as a lawyer but also as a father. You are my greatest achievement, and I am proud of the beautiful individuals you are becoming.

I extend a heartfelt thank you to my parents, whose guidance and belief in me have shaped the person I am today. Your insistence on the value of education and your push for me to pursue a career in law has been instrumental in my success. Your sacrifices, support, and love have not gone unnoticed, and I owe a significant part of my achievements to you.

To my brother, who has not only been a sibling but also a close friend, your strength and resilience in the face of adversity have been inspiring. The bond we share has been a constant reminder of the importance of family and the power of perseverance. Your journey to attend law school and dedication to your family have been motivating factors in my dedication to my family and the legal profession.

Lastly, I extend my thanks to the rest of my family, whose love and support have been unwavering. Your encouragement and belief in me have been sources of comfort and motivation. You have all played a vital role in my journey, and for that, I am immensely grateful.

This book is a culmination of not just my experiences but also the collective support and inspiration from each one of you. Thank you for being my guiding stars.

In extending my deepest gratitude, I cannot overlook the countless clients who have entrusted me with their legal battles over the years. To each and every one of you, I extend a heartfelt thank you. Your trust in me and my firm has not only been the foundation of my professional journey but has also profoundly impacted my personal growth.

Many of you have transitioned from being clients to cherished friends. Our continued connections, whether through the annual exchange of Christmas cards, interactions on social media, or personal conversations, are treasures I hold dear. These ongoing relationships are a constant reminder of the personal and human aspects of the legal profession.

Your stories, challenges, and triumphs have not only shaped my career but have also enriched my life in countless ways. Each case has been more than just a professional engagement; it has been an opportunity to connect, understand, and make a difference in someone's life.

The journey we embarked on together in seeking justice and resolution has often extended beyond the courtroom and legal documents. It has fostered a sense of community and mutual respect that I value immensely. The friendships that have blossomed from these professional relationships are a testament to the trust and bond we have built.

So, to all my past and present clients, thank you for choosing me as your legal representative and for the privilege of being a part of your life. Your confidence in me has been a driving force in my commitment to the legal profession, and for that, I am eternally grateful. The journey we have shared in navigating the complexities of the law has been both an honor and a profound responsibility that I have always held in the highest regard.

Contents

Chapter 1:
Walking in My Client's Shoes: A Personal Journey of Empathy and Advocacy

Growing up, I didn't have to imagine the stress, pain, and financial burden of an accident. I lived it.

When I was just a child, my brother's life was dramatically changed in the blink of an eye. While riding his bicycle, he was brutally struck by a car. The accident wasn't a fleeting incident, it left deep emotional scars that went beyond the physical ones. While he was eventually blessed with a full recovery, those days he spent in the hospital are etched into my memory. I remember the very real, very human struggle my family had to endure. I recall my parents fear of being buried in a mountain of medical bills and how this accident and my brother's revovery could effect them financially.

My brother and I together as children.

My brother was the best man at my wedding

This personal trauma resurfaced as an adult while traveling on Route 93 in New Hampshire. My two young sons sat beside me when our car was ruthlessly struck from behind. The sheer force was enough to total our vehicle. And while I came away with only stitches and head trauma, the emotional scars ran deeper. At that moment, I was taken back to my childhood, reliving the trauma and understanding the potential outcomes of such a harrowing event.

My vehicle after being struck from behind on Route 93 in NH

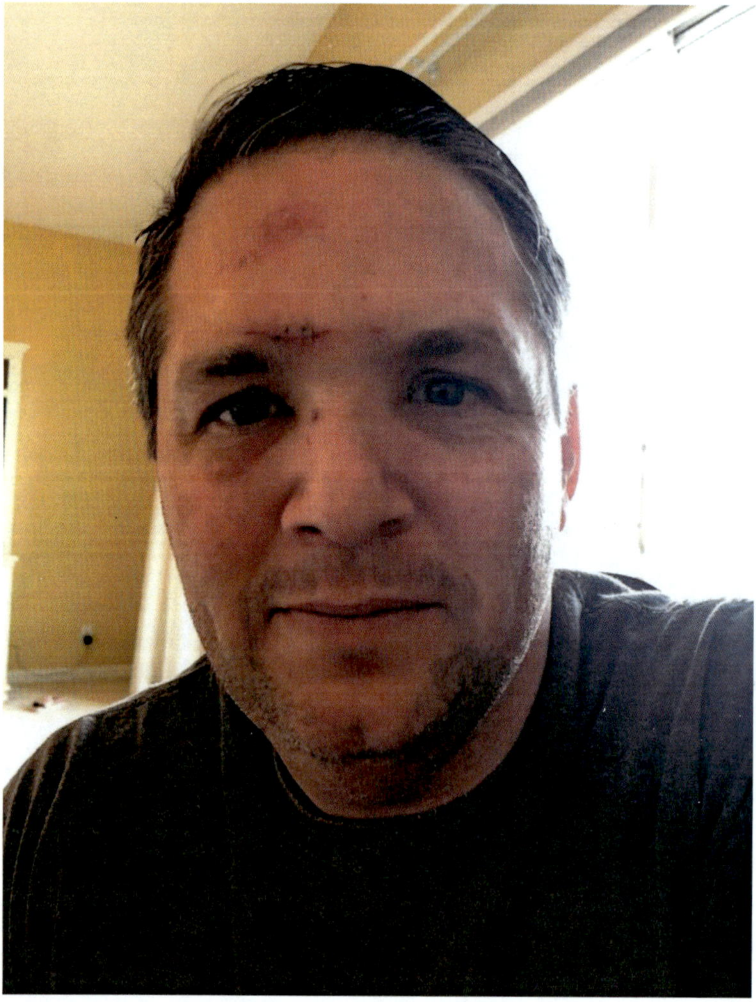

Injuries from the accident

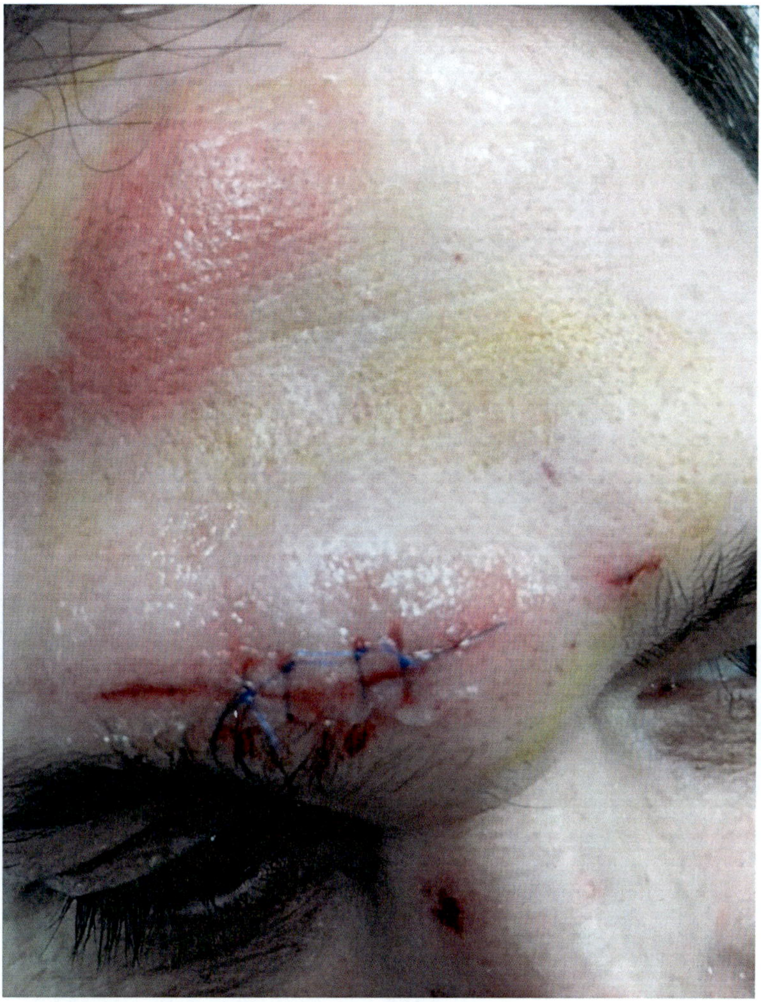

Facial injuries from the accident

But it's not just these direct experiences that have shaped my understanding and compassion. My familial history is riddled with tales of hardship and sacrifice. My grandparents, brave souls who immigrated to the United States, embarked on this journey with nothing but dreams of a better future. Yet, they were met with deplorable working conditions, where their well-being was a mere afterthought. Similarly, my father, a laborer in the construction industry, bore the brunt of needless injuries, which was a stark reminder of the cost of negligence and disregard for human safety.

My Father, as a young man working in Queens, NY at a construction site

Perhaps it was these stories, or perhaps it was my parent's own aspirations for me that set me on the path to law. I distinctly remember my father, weary after long hours at the construction site, handing me a 400-page legal textbook urging me to dive in. To him and my mother, the legal profession wasn't just about statutes and rulings. It was about creating a positive change for others. It was about having a tangible impact, about advocating for those who couldn't advocate for themselves.

Family Picture

Embracing this ethos, I began my legal journey championing the rights of employees, fighting tooth and nail for those unjustly fired or laid off. My commitment to my community also led me to serve as a prosecutor in district court, further deepening my understanding of the myriad ways the legal system impacts people's lives.

At its core, practicing law isn't about grand legal theories or convoluted statutes. It's about the people. It's about understanding their stories, empathizing with their pain, and striving for justice. My personal experiences, coupled with the legacies of my ancestors, have instilled in me a profound sense of purpose. I don't just represent my clients, I understand them because, in many ways, their stories are my own.

The hospital corridors where my brother lay recovering became all too familiar to our family. His bed became a stark reminder of the unpredictable fragility of life. But amid this trying period, a silver lining emerged. Watching my parents navigate the complexities of medical bills and insurance claims, I witnessed resilience, determination, and a deep sense of love. These early lessons taught me the value of perseverance in the face of adversity, a lesson I've carried with me throughout my legal career.

Later in life, when the cold metal of another vehicle crumpled against mine on Route 93, I felt a wave of fear, not just for myself but predominantly for my young boys. Those minutes post-accident, as we assessed our physical well-being and grappled with the immediate shock, memories of my brother's accident flooded back. The reality of our shared experiences bound us even more tightly as a family, emphasizing the importance of support systems.

These incidents, combined with the tales of my ancestors, painted a clear picture, life is filled with challenges, but with resilience and the right support, we can overcome them. My grandparents, having left everything familiar behind, worked tirelessly in their new homeland. Their dedication was a testament to the human spirit's ability to endure. My father, with his hands worn from manual labor, dreamt of a different life for his children, a life where they could use their minds and voices to bring about change.

My parent's dreams for me weren't rooted in a desire for prestige but in a profound understanding of the power of advocacy. The legal textbook they brought me wasn't just a book it was a symbol of hope, a promise of a future where I could make a difference. And with every page I turned, I absorbed not just legal jargon but the essence of justice and the importance of standing up for the voiceless.

As I transitioned into the legal world, I didn't see clients, I saw stories, struggles, and dreams. Each case wasn't just about winning in court, it was about restoring dignity, seeking justice, and ensuring a brighter future. Behind every case number was a narrative, a person, a family, mirroring my own experiences.

Today, as I stand with my clients, I don't stand as a distant professional. I stand as someone who has felt their pain, shared their fears, and understands the weight of their dreams. My journey, both personal and professional, is a testament to the belief that with empathy, dedication, and a fierce commitment to justice, we can not only navigate the complex world of personal injury but also find healing, hope, and a path forward.

Chapter 2:
Understanding Accidents and Their Aftermath

In the realm of personal injury law, the term "accident" refers to an unforeseen event that results in injury or harm to an individual. This event can be as commonplace as a slip and fall in a grocery store or as catastrophic as a multi-vehicle collision on the freeway. Often, these incidents are not purely accidental but are the consequences of someone's negligence or failure to act with reasonable care. Generally, an ordinary person is unaware of what measures they should take if they are involved in an accident.

There are several types of accidents that I will discuss in detail to help enable innocent victims to stand up for themselves.

Types of Accidents

Vehicle Accidents

Vehicle accidents encompass a range of incidents, from minor fender benders to catastrophic multi-car collisions, and represent a significant portion of personal injury cases. These accidents can occur due to a multitude of factors including, but not limited to, driver negligence (such as distracted driving, driving under the influence of alcohol or drugs, or speeding), environmental conditions (like icy roads or poor visibility), mechanical failures, or violations of traffic laws. The consequences of these accidents can vary dramatically, from temporary inconveniences and minor injuries to severe, long-term impairments or even fatalities. In my own accident where I was struck from behind, the driver never hit his brakes and was clearly distracted.

Truck Accidents

Truck accidents involving large vehicles like semis, 18-wheelers, and other commercial trucks are particularly devastating due to the sheer size and weight of these vehicles compared to standard passenger cars. The physics behind these crashes means that the impact is often severe, leading to significant property damage and catastrophic injuries or fatalities. The complexity of truck accidents is not just in their physical and medical impact but also in the legal and regulatory landscape that governs commercial trucking. One of the primary factors contributing to truck accidents is driver fatigue. Despite strict regulations governing the number of hours a truck driver can consecutively operate their vehicle, pressure to meet delivery deadlines can lead to drivers pushing beyond safe limits. Other factors include improper loading of cargo, which can lead to unbalanced trucks and loss of control, mechanical failures, especially concerning brakes and tires; and inadequate training or oversight of drivers. Environmental conditions, such as bad weather, can further exacerbate these risks. From a legal perspective, truck accidents can be more complicated than standard car accidents. Liability might extend beyond the truck driver to include the trucking company, contractors, employers, and insurance companies.

Establishing negligence may involve scrutinizing driver logs, maintenance records, and cargo loading procedures. Moreover, trucking companies often have robust legal teams and insurance coverage, making it imperative for victims to seek skilled legal representation to level the playing field.

The severity of injuries in truck accidents also means that victims often face long-term or permanent disabilities, requiring extensive medical treatment, rehabilitation, and ongoing care. The financial implications can be enormous, not just in terms of immediate medical expenses but also in long-term income loss, reduced earning capacity, and the need for life-long medical or personal care. Psychological impacts, such as PTSD, anxiety, and depression, are also common among truck accident victims and witnesses.

Motorcycle accidents

Motorcycle accidents, while sharing some similarities with car and truck accidents, come with their unique set of challenges and characteristics. Motorcycles, by design, lack the structural protections that enclosed vehicles offer. Without the buffer of doors, a roof, or other safety features, motorcyclists are more vulnerable to direct impact during collisions. This vulnerability means that even minor accidents can result in severe injuries or fatalities for motorcycle riders.

A range of factors can contribute to motorcycle accidents. Visibility issues top the list, as motorcycles' smaller profiles make them less noticeable to other motorists. This can lead to situations where drivers unintentionally cut off or pull out in front of motorcycles. Road hazards like potholes, wet surfaces, or gravel can also pose significant dangers to motorcyclists, who require a stable road surface for safe operation. Furthermore, some motorcycle accidents result from inexperienced or reckless riding, such as excessive speeding or unsafe lane changes.

Injuries sustained in motorcycle accidents are often profound. Road rash, a common injury, occurs when a rider slides across the pavement, leading to severe skin abrasions. Broken bones, traumatic brain injuries (even with helmet use), spinal injuries, and internal bleeding are also frequent outcomes. These injuries can have long-term or permanent repercussions, affecting a victim's ability to work, engage in daily activities, and enjoy a pre-accident quality of life.

The legal aspects of motorcycle accidents can sometimes be influenced by societal biases. Motorcyclists are often unfairly stereotyped as "risk-takers" or "daredevils," a perception that can affect jury decisions or insurance settlements. As such, establishing a clear narrative of the accident, backed by evidence, witness testimonies, and expert opinions, becomes paramount in securing fair compensation.

Given the severity and unique nature of motorcycle accidents, victims stand to benefit from specialized legal representation. An attorney experienced in motorcycle accident cases can navigate the nuances, challenge biases, and ensure that victims' rights are upheld, and they are compensated justly for their injuries and losses.

Dog Bites

Dog bites, while often underestimated in terms of their severity and impact, can constitute a significant portion of personal injury cases. These incidents range from minor nips to severe maulings and can have far-reaching consequences for both the victim and the dog owner. Understanding the legal, medical, and emotional facets of dog bite cases is crucial for anyone involved in such an incident.

The immediate concern in a dog bite incident is the physical injury, which can vary from superficial skin wounds to deep lacerations, punctures, and, in extreme cases, life-threatening injuries. Victims might require immediate medical attention to address bleeding, prevent infection, and, if necessary, perform surgery for severe wounds. Rabies vaccinations may be needed if the dog's vaccination history is unknown.

Beyond the physical injuries, dog bites can leave lasting psychological scars. Victims, especially children, may develop a phobia of dogs, suffer from post-traumatic stress disorder (PTSD), and experience anxiety and depression. Such emotional trauma can be as debilitating as the physical injuries and require professional psychological treatment.

Legally, dog bite cases fall under the umbrella of personal injury law but are distinct due to the involvement of animal behavior and differing laws across jurisdictions. Many states have enacted specific dog bite statutes, while others rely on the broader principles of negligence and liability. Some jurisdictions follow a "strict liability" doctrine, where a dog owner may be held liable for a dog bite even if the dog has never shown aggression or bitten someone before. Other areas might operate under a "one-bite rule," where an owner is only held responsible if they knew or should have known that their dog was likely to cause that type of injury.

Investigating a dog bite incident involves examining the circumstances of the bite, the dog's history, and the owner's actions. Was the dog provoked? Was the victim trespassing, or was he acting aggressively towards the dog? Did the owner take reasonable steps to prevent the dog from biting? Answers to these questions can significantly influence the outcome of a case.

The financial burden of a dog bite can be substantial, including medical bills, reconstructive surgery (in cases of severe wounds), lost wages, and counseling expenses. Victims may seek compensation through the homeowners' insurance policies of the dog owner or through legal action if insurance is not available or insufficient.

For dog owners, understanding their responsibilities and potential liabilities is crucial. Preventative measures, such as proper training, secure fencing, and socialization of the dog, can mitigate risks. Additionally, understanding the coverage of their insurance policy concerning dog bites is important for financial protection.

Dog bites represent a complex intersection of personal injury law, animal behavior, and community safety issues. For victims, addressing the full spectrum of injury, physical, psychological, and financial is vital. For dog owners, understanding and mitigating liability risks is equally important. In these cases, the counsel of an experienced personal injury attorney can be invaluable in navigating the legal intricacies and advocating for the rights and protections of those involved.

Slip and falls

Slip and fall accidents are among the most common causes of personal injury claims. These incidents occur when an individual slips, trips, or falls as a result of a hazardous or dangerous condition on someone else's property. They can happen anywhere from commercial properties like grocery stores and office buildings to private homes and even on public sidewalks. The nature of these accidents often seems deceptively simple, but the injuries and legal complexities they can engender are anything but.

Slips and falls can be caused by a variety of conditions such as wet floors, uneven surfaces, poorly lit staircases, ice or snow accumulations, and unexpected obstacles are just a few examples. The injuries from these falls range from minor bruises and scrapes to more serious injuries like fractures, head injuries, and spinal cord trauma, and, in severe cases, can even be fatal. The severity of the injury may depend on multiple factors, such as the age and physical condition of the victim and the nature of the fall.

From a legal standpoint, slip and fall cases fall under the broader category of premises liability claims. Property owners (or, in some cases, renters or those in control of the property) have a legal duty to keep their premises reasonably safe and free of hazards. When an accident occurs, one of the key considerations is whether the property owner acted negligently, did they know about the dangerous condition and failed to address it? Or should they have reasonably known about it?

Determining liability in these cases can be complicated. It often hinges on nuances. The distinction between a 'transitory' foreign substance in a business establishment (like a spilled liquid) versus a permanent hazardous condition (like a broken stair), the specific laws and codes pertaining to the property, and even the actions of the victim at the time of the accident (such as ignoring warning signs).

For victims, the impact of a slip-and-fall accident can extend far beyond physical injuries. There may be substantial medical bills, lost wages due to time off work, long-term rehabilitation costs, and significant pain and suffering. In cases of severe injuries, victims may face life-altering consequences, including long-term or permanent disability.

Navigating the aftermath of a slip and fall requires careful consideration of several factors. Documenting the accident scene, gathering witness statements, and securing medical documentation are crucial early steps. Dealing with property owners and their insurance companies can also be challenging, as they may quickly try to deny liability or offer settlements that fall short of covering the full extent of damages.

Workplace accidents

Workplace accidents encompass a wide range of injuries and hazards occurring in the course of employment. These incidents can happen in any type of work environment, from construction sites and manufacturing plants to offices and retail stores. The nature of these accidents can vary significantly, including falls, equipment-related injuries, exposure to harmful substances, repetitive motion injuries, and even incidents of violence. The implications of such accidents are substantial, affecting employees, employers, and the broader economy.

Workplace accidents often result from a combination of unsafe working conditions, inadequate training, mechanical failures, and human error. These can occur due to wet floors, uneven surfaces, or improper use of ladders.

When we talk about accidents involving machinery, especially in places like manufacturing or construction sites, they can be pretty serious. We're not just talking about small cuts or bruises here, we're looking at really severe stuff like amputations or, in the worst cases, even fatalities.

And then there's the issue of lifting heavy stuff or doing the same motions over and over again. You know, that can really do a number on your body, leading to strains, sprains, or even long-term problems with your muscles and bones.

Oh, and let's not forget about hazardous materials. Working around toxic chemicals or in harmful environments can be really risky. Sometimes you don't even notice the health problems right away, they can show up much later.

Plus, there's workplace violence to consider. It's pretty alarming, but aggression and violence in the workplace, whether it's coming from coworkers or someone from outside the workplace, can cause both physical and mental harm. It's a real concern in any job environment.In most jurisdictions, workplace accidents are predominantly governed by workers' compensation laws. These laws are designed to provide injured workers with prompt medical treatment and financial compensation for lost wages, irrespective of who was at fault for the accident. In return, employers are typically shielded from private lawsuits by employees over these injuries.

However, there can be exceptions in certain jurisdictions, particularly in cases of gross negligence or when a third party (someone other than the employer or co-worker) is responsible for the injury. In such cases, injured employees might have the right to file a personal injury lawsuit outside of the workers' compensation system.

The aftermath of a workplace accident can be challenging for the injured worker. Immediate concerns include receiving medical attention and reporting the injury to the employer as soon as possible. Understanding workers' compensation benefits, rights under employment laws, and potentially applicable disability laws is crucial.

For employers, workplace accidents highlight the importance of rigorous health and safety policies, regular training, and adherence to occupational safety regulations. Not only do these measures help prevent accidents and ensure a safer working environment, but they also minimize the risk of legal liabilities and financial losses associated with workplace accidents.

Defective products

Defective products are items that, due to errors in design, manufacturing, or labeling, pose a risk of injury to consumers. These products can range from small household appliances to large automobiles, and the defects can lead to minor injuries or, in worst-case scenarios, significant harm or even death. Understanding the complexities surrounding defective products is essential for both consumers and manufacturers, particularly regarding legal liability, consumer safety, and regulatory compliance.

When it comes to products that don't work the way they should, you usually run into three main problems. First up, there are design defects. This is like, imagine you buy a chair that looks cool but has a design that makes it topple over easily. It's not about how it's made, it's just designed in a risky way right from the get-go. So even if it's built perfectly, following the design to a T, it's still going to be unsafe to sit on.

Then, you have manufacturing defects. This is different because it's about how the product is made, not designed. Think of it like this, you have a recipe for a great, safe-to-use lawn mower, but somewhere along the line in making it, something goes wrong. Maybe a part isn't fitted right, or a safety feature is left out. So, even though the design is solid, the final product that comes out of the factory ends up being dangerous.

Lastly, there's what they call marketing defects, but it's really about failing to warn people. This happens when a product doesn’t come with the right instructions or warnings. Like, if you buy a powerful cleaning chemical that doesn’t have a label telling you to wear gloves, you might end up with a nasty skin burn. It's not that there's something wrong with the product's design or how it's made, it's that you weren't given the heads-up on how to use it safely.

In most jurisdictions, the law of product liability is the primary legal framework that deals with defective or dangerous products. This law aims to protect consumers from unsafe products and hold manufacturers, distributors, wholesalers, and retailers accountable for putting such products into the hands of consumers.

For consumers, the first line of defense against defective products is staying informed about recalls and safety warnings. However, if injury occurs, they may have the right to seek compensation. The injured party must demonstrate that the product was defective, that the defect caused their injury, and that they were using the product as intended.

Compensation in defective product cases may cover medical expenses, lost wages, pain and suffering, and, in cases of wrongful death, additional damages. In certain cases, punitive damages might also be awarded, especially if the manufacturer's behavior in producing or selling the defective product is deemed particularly reckless or malicious. Manufacturers must ensure their products are safe for consumer use, which involves rigorous testing, quality control, and adhering to industry and governmental standards and regulations. When a defect is identified, they are responsible for issuing recalls and providing remedies to consumers, which could include repairs, replacements, or refunds.

Defective product cases underscore the importance of safety, responsibility, and legal diligence for all parties involved. For consumers, they highlight the need for awareness and the right to compensation in the event of injury. For manufacturers, these cases serve as a reminder of the paramount importance of product safety and the potentially grave legal and financial consequences of negligence or oversights in the design, production, or marketing processes.

Medical Malpractice

Medical malpractice occurs when a healthcare provider be it a doctor, nurse, therapist, or other medical personnel, deviates from the standards of their profession, resulting in harm to a patient. This form of professional negligence is a critical area of personal injury law, given its potential to cause significant, long-lasting damage to patients and their families. Medical malpractice cases are among the most complex in personal injury law due to the intricate nature of medicine and the legal nuances involved.

When it comes to medical malpractice claims, there are a few key things that need to be proven. First off, there has to be a clear patient-doctor relationship. This just means that the doctor agreed to treat you, and you agreed to be treated. It's like a promise that the doctor will take care of you. Next, we need to show that the doctor didn't quite do their job right, according to what's expected in their field. Picture this, if most doctors would act one way under certain circumstances, but your doctor did something totally different, that could be a problem. It's like if you're supposed to drive on the right side of the road, but someone decides to drive on the left and causes an accident. It's not following the rules of the road, or in this case, the rules of medicine. Then, there's the issue of causation. This is all about connecting the dots, proving that the doctor's slip-up directly caused harm. It's like saying, "Because you drove on the wrong side, there was a crash, and someone got hurt."

Finally, there's the part about damages. This isn't just about physical injuries, it can also mean financial or emotional harm. So, if the doctor's mistake led to extra medical bills, lost work time, or emotional distress, that counts. It's like showing the consequences of that car crash, hospital bills, time off work, the mental stress of the whole thing and asking for it to be made right.

Alright, let's break down medical malpractice into simpler terms. Think of it like a bunch of different ways a doctor or hospital can mess up, and each one can seriously affect your health. It's kind of like a variety of mishaps that can happen in healthcare, each with its own set of problems.

Think about misdiagnosis or delayed diagnosis first. It's like going to a mechanic because your car's making a strange noise, but they say it's all good, and then your car breaks down later. In the medical world, if a doctor doesn't figure out what's wrong with you or takes too long, you might miss out on getting the right treatment at the right time.

Then there are surgical errors. Imagine if you took your car in to get the brakes fixed, but the mechanic worked on the transmission instead. In surgery, this could be something as serious as operating on the wrong part of your body or leaving a tool inside after they close you up.

Medication errors are another big issue. This is like if someone gave you the wrong instructions for a product and you ended up using it all wrong. In medicine, it means getting the wrong medicine or the wrong dose, which can be really dangerous.

Childbirth injuries are particularly tough. This could happen if a doctor doesn't take care of the mother and the baby properly during delivery, leading to injuries. It's a very sensitive area because it's about bringing new life into the world.

Then there's the failure to treat. Say you know something's wrong with your car, the mechanic knows it too, but they just don't fix it. In healthcare, it's like a doctor knowing what's wrong with you but not giving you the treatment you need.

Lastly, there's medical product liability. This is about problems with medical devices or products, kind of like if a safety feature in your car was faulty and caused an accident.

These malpractice cases can get pretty complex. They often involve lots of medical details and need experts to explain things. It's also tricky to figure out if a doctor just made a simple mistake or really messed up. Plus, there's a whole bunch of legal and medical stuff you need to know to make a case. And to top it all off, you've got to start your case within a certain time frame, or you might lose your chance to do anything about it.

The consequences of medical malpractice for patients can be devastating, including permanent disability, additional medical treatments, loss of income, and emotional trauma. For medical professionals and institutions, besides financial and reputational damage, malpractice cases can lead to increased scrutiny and changes in practices.

Medical malpractice remains a critical issue in the healthcare system, reflecting the delicate balance between patient safety and the realities of medical practice. For victims, understanding their rights and the mechanisms for seeking redress is essential. For healthcare providers, these cases underscore the importance of maintaining the highest standards of care and continually updating skills and knowledge. Effectively addressing medical malpractice demands a concerted effort from both legal and medical professions, focusing on patient safety, professional accountability, and equitable resolution of disputes.

Bringing a medical malpractice case isn't exactly a walk in the park, and there are a couple of big hurdles that often come up. First, let's talk about the cost. Going for a medical malpractice lawsuit can be like deciding to renovate your entire house, it's expensive. There are all sorts of costs that pile up, lawyer fees, the cost of getting medical records, paying for expert witnesses... the list goes on. Sometimes, even just starting the case feels like you're putting a down payment on a fancy new car. It's a big financial commitment, and there's no guarantee of winning, which makes it a bit of a risky investment.

Then, there's the challenge of finding another doctor to speak up against the one you're suing. It's kind of like trying to find a coach who's willing to critique another coach's playbook in front of everyone. Doctors, like many professionals, often don't want to go against their own. They might know each other, work in the same circles, or just not want to get involved in a legal battle. So, getting a medical expert to say, "Yep, this doctor messed up," can be really tough. It's not just about finding someone who thinks there was a mistake, it's about finding someone who's willing to say it, on record, and stick by it all the way to court.

All in all, pursuing a medical malpractice case can feel like you're climbing a mountain without the right gear. It's costly, it's complex, and it requires finding just the right people to back you up. Hiring the right law firm is of the utmost importance in this field of law.

Chapter 3:
Immediate Steps After an Accident

Accidents are like uninvited guests that bring chaos into an otherwise orderly life. For anyone who has experienced an accident, the moments and days following the event are a critical period that can shape their recovery journey and impact their legal rights. As a personal injury attorney, I have seen first-hand how the actions taken immediately after an accident can make a substantial difference in the outcome of a personal injury case. This chapter is dedicated to guiding you through those initial steps so you can protect both. An accident is undoubtedly a traumatic experience for all those involved. It can leave physical and emotional scars. The physical scars can heal in time, but the emotional scars do not always go away that easily.

Your adrenaline levels will surge immediately after an accident, which can both sharpen and cloud your judgment. Take a deep breath and try to assess your surroundings. Are you in immediate danger from oncoming traffic or a potential fire? Is it safe to exit your vehicle, or is staying put the safer option?

If the area is hazardous, such as in the middle of heavy traffic or on a blind curve, consider what measures you can take to alert oncoming vehicles. Turn on your hazard lights and, if you have them, set up warning triangles or flares at a safe distance behind your vehicle to prevent further collisions. When you get into an accident, the most important thing is never to panic. Safety always comes first. Your life and the lives of those involved are what matters most. Try to remain calm and cool and try to step away from the accident situation to recollect your thoughts about what happened.

Check yourself for injuries before moving to ensure you do not exacerbate any potential harm. If you're injured, try to remain calm and wait for emergency services to arrive. If others are injured, and you are able to help, do so with caution, as moving someone improperly can worsen their injuries. Even if there are no apparent serious injuries, calling 911 is essential. Report the accident and follow the dispatcher's instructions. Remember, some injuries, especially internal ones, may not show immediate symptoms.

If you're physically able to, begin documenting the scene. Take photographs of your vehicle, the surrounding area, any other vehicles involved, and your injuries. Our law firm offers a smartphone app for iPhone and Android devices that can be used to help in this process. With the app, you can find emergency services near your accident scene, make your own accident report with pictures and videos of the accident, input the contact information for the other driver and witnesses, mark the exact location using GPS, record your out-of-pocket expenses, journal about your recovery and much more. You can download our app here (https://apps.apple.com/us/app/dibella-law-offices-injury-app/id1579741060) or visit www.everycaseispersonal.com scroll to the bottom of the homepage and scan the QR code.

Exchange insurance information with the other driver, but limit your conversation about the accident. Avoid admitting fault or making statements that could be used against you later. Not all drivers may be cooperative in providing their information. If they are unwilling, it would be ideal to get a photo of the driver and their license plate if possible. This gives you an additional layer of security because photographic evidence should be enough for you to prove who the driver involved was.

You have to always protect yourself in all circumstances, so you should never admit guilt or even apologize because that could be used against you at a later time to indicate that you were the guilty party. If there are witnesses, collect their contact information. Their testimony can be invaluable in piecing together the accident's narrative. You should request their personal information, which would include at least names and phone numbers in case you require their assistance later. You should let them know that you will contact them when you require their assistance. Eyewitnesses can help corroborate your story in case the guilty party leaves the scene or tries to make up a story.

Even if you've refused medical treatment at the scene or feel that your injuries are minor, it's prudent to visit an emergency room or your doctor for a thorough check-up. Document every visit, treatment, and prescription, as this information can be important to your claim. Report the accident to your insurance company as soon as possible. Provide them with the facts, but be cautious about making any declarations or signing any releases without consulting your attorney.

Maintaining detailed records after an accident is crucial. This includes a log of conversations you have about the accident, all correspondence with your insurance company, receipts for all expenses incurred due to the accident, and documentation of any time missed from work. Our office provides each new client with a journal so that they can document their recovery, calendar appointments or keep track of expenses. It is harder than you think to remember what happened weeks after an accident or after a doctor's appointment. A best practice would be to journal in real-time as you have a doctor's appointment, incur medical expenses, or any particular worth noting related to the accident. If you can not keep track in real time because life can get busy for all of us, it is a good idea to pick one day of the week when you have some free time to journal about how the week was and any experiences you had related to the accident.

Request a copy of the police report as it serves as an official account of the accident. Review it for accuracy and understand the information it contains, as it will be a key piece of evidence in any claim or lawsuit. When the police arrive on the scene, please ensure you are responding honestly to their questions and inform them that you may feel alright now but could feel hurt later, too. It is best to make sure they are aware of all your disclaimers. You should also make sure that the officer provides you with his name, designation, department, and incident number. You should take photographic evidence of all the surrounding areas, streets, obstacles, structures, and car positions associated with the accident so your information corroborates with the pictures the police took when you later speak with an attorney and/or insurance agent.

Consult a personal injury attorney as soon as you're able to. Most offer free consultations and can provide you with guidance on your next steps. They can help interpret the police report, advise on communication with insurers, and provide direction for keeping records of your injuries and expenses. It would be best if you got in touch with an attorney first before you speak with the insurance company. Insurance companies will often try to take a recorded statement from you. These statements may be obtained at a later date to try to impeach any inconsistencies from the first recorded statements with any current testimony.

Hiring an attorney may help you avoid all the mental stress that comes along with fighting insurance companies, dealing with collection firms, gathering medical records and bills, and fighting to reduce liens. There can be several ways to prove to an insurance company or in court how an accident has impaired your physical ability, caused you mental stress, anxiety, anguish, and even loss of livelihood. Personal injury cases can be highly complex, so an attorney who knows how best to get you the right damages is critical.

Your attorney will explain how the insurance claim process works, starting with an investigation into the accident. They will help you gather necessary evidence, including witness statements, expert testimony, and accident reconstruction if needed. Your attorney will also handle communication with insurance adjusters, who are trained to minimize the company's payout. Your lawyer will negotiate to ensure that you receive a fair settlement that covers your medical expenses, lost wages, and pain and suffering.

The initial actions you take after an accident are crucial and can significantly impact the eventual outcome of your personal injury claim. By following these guidelines, you can protect your health and rights while laying the foundation for a strong legal case. Remember, the goal is not just to recover from the accident but also to ensure that you're not left struggling with its financial aftermath. The journey to recovery can be a challenging one, but with the right steps and support, you can navigate through it toward a resolution that brings peace of mind and justice for your suffering.

It is also essential to understand how insurance premiums work when a car accident happens.

According to bankrate.com (Kim, 2023):

> "Car insurance rates typically tend to go up after an accident, but more notably after an at-fault accident. Since insurance companies calculate premiums based on risk, having an at-fault accident on your driving record may

cause insurers to see you as a higher risk to insure. If you are deemed higher risk, it is likely that your premiums will increase. However, there are several factors that determine the exact amount that your premium will increase. Factors like your auto insurance provider, driving record, claims history, geographic location, and, in some states, even your age and gender are looked at when determining the exact rate you pay. Young drivers may see the highest increases after an accident since insurers typically view them as an especially risky group to insure."[1]

Bankrate.com (Kim, 2023) provides us with the following premium statistics:

	Average annual premium for full coverage	Average annual premium for minimum coverage
Before an accident	$2,014	$622
After an at-fault accident	$2,854	$892
Difference	42%	43%

[1] Kim, G. (2023, October 18). *How much will my car insurance go up after an accident?* Bankrate. https://www.bankrate.com/insurance/car/rates-after-an-accident/

Experienced and qualified attorneys can help you with all the insurance claim paperwork so you get adequate compensation and protect yourself from your premiums rising too high.

Finally, don't post on social media about your accident/injuries! I know it is common for many of us today to live much of our lives on social media. However, when it comes to your accident and injuries, you do not want to allow certain pictures or statements to be taken out of context. For example, you may have really hurt your arm. A picture of you at a gym may bring unwanted questions about what you were doing there, even if you went there just to walk around a track or to sit in a steam room. You do not want unnecessary attention. Social media allows people to judge your situation, criticize, or try to draw incorrect assumptions. You are opening yourself up to scrutiny that may be taken out of context. Social media posts are often obtained in litigation and can be used against you in a legal case down the road.

Let's consider a few hypothetical scenarios where poor use of social media after an accident could negatively impact your case:

<u>Scenario 1: Posting About Physical Activities</u>

Hypothesis: Jane was in a car accident and suffered a back injury. She files a personal injury lawsuit claiming severe pain and limited mobility. However, a week after the accident, she posts pictures on Instagram from a hiking trip, smiling and carrying a heavy backpack.

Impact: The defendant's legal team finds these posts and uses them to argue that Jane's injuries are not as severe as claimed. This contradicts her statements about her physical limitations and can significantly weaken her case.

Scenario 2: Contradictory Statements

Hypothesis: John reports severe mental anguish and emotional trauma after a workplace accident. He files a claim for emotional distress. However, his Facebook profile shows frequent posts about going out with friends, attending parties, and enjoying life, all marked with timestamps after his accident.

Impact: The defense uses these posts to challenge John's claims of emotional distress, suggesting that his social media activity does not align with someone suffering from severe mental trauma. This can cast doubt on the credibility of his claim.

Scenario 3: Inconsistencies in Accident Details

Hypothesis: Emily tweets right after a slip-and-fall accident at a store, exaggerating some details of the incident. In her lawsuit, however, her account of the accident, based on more careful reflection, differs from her initial impulsive tweet.

Impact: The defense brings up this discrepancy, using the tweet to question Emily's reliability and the accuracy of her claims. This inconsistency can harm her credibility and weaken her lawsuit.

Scenario 4: Discussing the Case Publicly

Hypothesis: Alex, involved in a motorcycle accident, frequently discusses his ongoing lawsuit details on Facebook, criticizing the other party and the legal process, and revealing information about settlement discussions.

Impact: Such public discussion can breach confidentiality agreements, complicate the legal process, and may be used by the opposing counsel to portray Alex as uncooperative or malicious. It could also influence the jury's perception if the case goes to trial.

These hypothetical scenarios underscore the importance of being cautious with social media use after an accident, especially when a legal case is involved. Posts that contradict injury claims, show a lack of seriousness about the incident, or reveal too much information can all be detrimental to a personal injury case. It's often wise to limit social media activity and consult with an attorney on best practices during an ongoing lawsuit.

Chapter 4: Gathering Essential Evidence

Our legal system works on proof and pieces of evidence. Therefore, evidence-gathering is absolutely essential. No matter how much you feel you have a strong case, it is weak without evidence. Otherwise, it becomes a case of "he said, she said." As an attorney, I understand firsthand how important it is to gather as much evidence as possible as quickly as possible in order to maximize your recovery months and years later. If you want justice, you must know how our legal system works.

In the complex and often overwhelming world of personal injury law, the power of concrete evidence cannot be overstated. This chapter aims to empower you, the accident victim, with the knowledge and tools necessary to gather and preserve crucial evidence meticulously. From photos and videos to medical records and police reports, each piece plays a pivotal role in establishing the facts of your case and ensuring your rights are protected.

In the context of a civil lawsuit, "evidence" refers to any material or information that is used to prove or disprove facts related to the case. For a layperson, it's helpful to think of evidence as the building blocks that help paint a clear picture of what happened in the situation being disputed.

When talking about evidence in a civil lawsuit, there's a whole mix of stuff that can come into play. First off, you've got your physical evidence, which is pretty straightforward. These are things you can actually touch, like items from the scene, documents, or even photos. Then, there's testimonial evidence. This is where people come in to tell their side of the story or what they saw happen. Documentary evidence includes all the paperwork, think emails, contracts, or medical records. And let's not forget digital evidence. We're talking about stuff from your gadgets, like text messages, social media posts, or even GPS data from your phone or car.

The reason all this evidence stuff matters is because it helps to either back up or challenge what everyone's saying in court. It's like putting together pieces of a puzzle so the judge or jury can get the full picture and make a decision that makes sense. But here's the catch, not just anything can be thrown in as evidence. It's got to be relevant, which means it needs to be directly related to what the lawsuit is about. Plus, it has to be gathered and used in a way that's above board, following all the legal rules.

Let's say you're in a personal injury case. The kind of evidence that might come up could be your medical records to show how hurt you got, pictures of where the accident happened, or people who actually saw it go down. Now, if we're talking about a disagreement over a contract, you'd probably see a bunch of emails being tossed around, the contract itself, and any money documents that are tied to it.

The bottom line is, evidence is like the backbone of your case. It's what helps figure out the real story behind all the legal talk, pointing out who's at fault and what should be done about it. It's all about getting to the truth of the matter and making sure the outcome is fair based on what really happened. Let's look at some hypothetical scenarios to illustrate why certain pieces of evidence in a legal case might or might not be admissible in court.

<u>Scenario 1: Surveillance Footage</u>

Hypothesis: In a slip-and-fall case at a shopping mall, the plaintiff's attorney wants to use surveillance footage showing the fall. However, the defense argues that the footage is unclear and does not show the specific area where the plaintiff fell.

Admissibility: The surveillance footage may be admissible if it is clear enough to show the conditions that led to the fall and can be authenticated (proven to be unaltered and from the correct time and place). However, if the footage is too blurry or doesn't clearly show the incident, it might be deemed inadmissible for not being relevant or for being overly prejudicial if it unfairly influences the jury without adding factual clarity.

<u>Scenario 2: Social Media Posts</u>

Hypothesis: In a personal injury case, the defense discovers social media posts by the plaintiff engaging in physical activities despite claiming severe injuries. The plaintiff claims these posts are old and not relevant to the current injury.

Admissibility: The social media posts can be admissible if the timestamps and content are relevant to the period after the injury occurred, showing a contradiction in the plaintiff's claims. However, if the posts are from before the accident or can be proven to be unrelated to the claimed injuries, they may be deemed inadmissible.

<u>Scenario 3: Witness Testimony About a Conversation</u>

Hypothesis: A witness wants to testify about a conversation they overheard where the defendant admitted fault for an accident. The defense argues this is hearsay and should not be allowed.

Admissibility: Generally, hearsay (an out-of-court statement made by someone other than the testifying witness) is not admissible. However, there are exceptions, such as if the statement is an admission by a party-opponent. In this case, if the witness overheard the defendant admitting fault, it could potentially be admissible under the hearsay exception.

<u>Scenario 4: Expert Testimony</u>

Hypothesis: In a medical malpractice case, the plaintiff's lawyer wants to bring in an expert witness to testify about the standard of care. The defense argues that the expert's field of specialization is different from that of the defendant doctor.

Admissibility: The expert testimony is likely admissible if the expert has relevant knowledge, skill, experience, training, or education that can help the jury understand the evidence or determine a fact in issue. However, if the expert's expertise is not directly relevant to the specific medical practices in question, their testimony might be deemed inadmissible.

These scenarios highlight that the admissibility of evidence largely depends on its relevance, reliability, and whether it adheres to specific legal rules and standards. Each piece of evidence must be scrutinized for its direct connection to the case and its ability to provide clarity without causing unfair prejudice or misleading the jury.

You can collect evidence and submit photographs and videos via the DiBella Law iPhone/Android app. Yes, we now have a handy app so that you can exchange important evidence with the push of a button!

You know, in this digital age we're living in, snapping photos and videos can really make a difference, especially after an accident. Thank goodness for smartphones! It's like they say, a picture is worth a thousand words. So, if you find yourself in a situation like a car crash or any kind of accident, getting out your phone and taking a bunch of pictures and videos can be a game-changer for your case.

Right after the accident, as soon as you know it's safe, start taking photos and videos of everything around you. Get the whole scene in there, like where it happened and what it looks like, and then zoom in on the nitty-gritty details. If it's a car accident, you'll want shots of all the cars from different angles, the traffic lights, how the road looks, and even the little things like debris or tire marks.

And don't forget about your injuries. It might sound a bit gruesome, but snapping pics of your injuries right after the accident and then as they heal can really show how bad things were and how they've affected you. Also, think about stuff like the weather, the lighting, or anything else around that might have played a role in what happened.

Just a heads up, though when you're playing photographer, remember to respect the law and other people's privacy. Don't get in the way of any official investigations and try not to invade anyone else's personal space.

While it might be tempting to share your experience on social media, it’s crucial to consider the potential legal ramifications. When in doubt, the safest approach is to keep details of your legal case off social media platforms.

Alright, let's break down what it means to get your medical records in a personal injury case and why it's super important. Imagine your medical records as the hard evidence that shows exactly how you got hurt and what it's taken to patch you up. These records are like the cornerstone of your case, they put numbers and facts to your injury and treatment.

So, first things first, after you get into an accident, it's key to get medical help right away. Not just because, you know, it's good for your health, but also because it starts the clock on documenting your injuries. Everything from your first visit to the doctor, to all the treatments and pills, gets recorded, and this stuff is gold for your case. But here's where it gets a bit administrative, you gotta ask for these records yourself or through your attorney if you have one. For each doctor, hospital, or clinic you visit, you'll need to make a formal request to get your hands on these records. Sometimes they'll charge a few bucks for copying and all, but it's worth it.

Also, there's this thing called HIPAA. Basically, it's a set of rules to keep your medical info private. When you're asking for your records, you gotta make sure everything's done by the book, respecting these privacy laws. Now, while you're getting treated, it's a smart move to keep your own notes. Like, jot down how you're feeling, what hurts, how the treatment's going, all of that. It's a great way to track your progress and also gives a more personal side to your story when you take it to court. It's like keeping a diary of your road to getting better.

But wait, there's more! Your case might need some extra types of evidence too. If there were people who saw the accident, their statements could really help. And sometimes, you might need an expert, like an accident reconstructionist or a doctor, to chime in with their professional opinion on what happened or how badly you're hurt.

If you lost work or money because of the accident, keeping a record of that is important too. Pay stubs, job records, all that stuff shows how the accident hit your wallet. And don't forget about any physical stuff you can show, like broken bits from a car crash or the actual product if it's a defective product case. Sometimes, you can even find helpful stuff from surveillance footage, like from traffic or security cameras. And in today's world, you never know what might pop up on social media that could help (or hurt) your case. So, gathering evidence isn't just about snapping pictures or grabbing your medical records. It's about piecing together the whole story from different angles, what you saw and felt, what others saw, and what the official records and experts say. It's like being a detective for your own case.

Let's walk through some hypothetical scenarios that show how clients can effectively gather various types of evidence for their personal injury cases:

<u>Scenario 1: Car Accident</u>

Client's Action: After a car accident, Sarah uses her smartphone to take photos of the vehicles, the road conditions, traffic signs, and any visible injuries. She also records a video to capture the flow of traffic and any skid marks or debris. She notes down the time and weather conditions. Sarah then collects contact information from witnesses and asks if anyone else took photos or videos. Later, she requests a copy of the police report and gathers all her medical records related to the accident.

Scenario 2: Slip and Fall at a Store

Client's Action: John slips and falls in a grocery store. He quickly takes photos of the spill that caused his fall, the surrounding area, and any absence of warning signs. He notes the time and any employees or customers who witnessed the fall. John asks the store manager for access to surveillance footage. After seeking medical attention, he keeps a detailed diary of his injuries, pain levels, and how the injury impacts his daily activities.

Scenario 3: Workplace Injury

Client's Action: Maria suffers an injury due to a faulty machine at work. She photographs the machine, focusing on the defective part, and captures the work area to show lack of safety measures. She collects statements from coworkers who witnessed the accident and gathers maintenance records of the equipment from her employer. Maria keeps all medical documents and maintains a journal of her recovery process, noting days off work and any lost wages.

Scenario 4: Medical Malpractice

Client's Action: After experiencing complications from a surgery, David requests his medical records, including surgery notes, from the hospital. He seeks a second opinion from another doctor, who points out inconsistencies in treatment. David records a timeline of his treatment, noting when he first noticed complications. He also maintains a diary detailing his post-surgery pain, challenges, and how the complications affect his life.

Scenario 5: Defective Product Injury

In each of these scenarios, the clients are proactive in collecting evidence immediately after the incident and during their recovery. By capturing visual evidence, securing documentation, and maintaining detailed personal records, they build a comprehensive case to support their personal injury claims. This proactive approach not only helps in establishing the facts but also in illustrating the full impact of the injury on their lives.

Chapter 5:
Knowing Your Rights

Understanding and exercising your rights after an accident is paramount in protecting your interests, both legally and health-wise. The immediate aftermath of an accident can be chaotic and overwhelming, but knowing your rights during this critical time can significantly impact the outcomes of your physical recovery and any potential legal proceedings.

In this essential chapter, we explore three fundamental areas that are crucial for anyone involved in an accident, the critical nature of statute of limitations, the imperative of seeking prompt medical care, and the complex principle of comparative negligence which applies in some jurisdictions. Each of these elements plays a vital role in safeguarding your rights and ensuring a fair and equitable resolution post-accident. We will delve into the importance of knowing the statute of limitations for your type of case and how they can significantly influence the course of your legal proceedings. We'll also discuss the importance of timely medical attention, not only for the sake of your health but also for its role in legal documentation and claim substantiation. Finally, we will unravel the often intricate concept of comparative negligence, a key factor in determining liability and the extent of potential compensation. Understanding these areas is crucial for effectively navigating the aftermath of an accident and for protecting your legal rights and interests.

The term “statute of limitations” refers to the law that sets a deadline for filing a lawsuit in the civil court system after an incident or injury. This time limit varies depending on the type of case and the jurisdiction in which the incident occurred. Once this period expires, the injured party loses the right to file a legal claim seeking damages for their injuries or losses. Let’s talk about the statute of limitations in Massachusetts and how you can find similar information for your own state. Think of the statute of limitations as a countdown clock. It starts ticking from the day you get injured or realize you’ve been harmed, and once time runs out, you can’t bring a lawsuit anymore.

In Massachusetts, for example, you usually have three years to file a personal injury lawsuit. That means if you’re in a car accident or slip and fall, you’ve got three years from the date of the accident to get your lawsuit in gear. Now, for medical malpractice cases, it’s a bit trickier and you should consult an attorney to determine exact deadlines. In Massachusetts you’ve still got three years, but the clock starts ticking from when you knew or should have discovered the negligence that caused the injury, which could be later than when it actually happened. However, there’s a catch, you can’t file more than seven years after the actual malpractice, regardless of when you discovered the injury.

Now, if you’re in another state and wondering, "What's the deal with the statute of limitations here?" a good starting point is your state government's website. Just hop on the internet, type in your state’s name followed by “statute of limitations,” and you should find some official government pages with the info you need. Another great resource is your state's bar association website. They often have easy-to-understand info about laws in your state, including the statute of limitations.

If you're still scratching your head or the legal jargon feels like a foreign language, it might be time to chat with a local attorney. They're the experts and can tell you exactly how much time you've got to file a lawsuit based on your specific situation. Remember, these time limits can be strict, so it's better to get the ball rolling sooner rather than later if you think you've got a case.

Let's consider a few hypothetical scenarios illustrating the consequences of not paying attention to the statute of limitations in legal cases:

Scenario 1: Car Accident Claim

Hypothesis: Tom was in a car accident and sustained injuries. He focused on his recovery and assumed he could file a lawsuit at any time. Two years and six months passed, and Tom finally decided to seek legal action, only to discover that the statute of limitations for personal injury claims in his state was two years. As a result, his lawsuit was dismissed, and he was unable to claim compensation for his injuries.

Scenario 2: Medical Malpractice Case

Hypothesis: Emily underwent surgery, and complications arose due to what she suspected was a surgical error. She spent a lot of time contemplating whether to sue, conducting her own research, and waiting for her condition to improve. By the time she contacted a lawyer, four years had passed. The statute of limitations for medical malpractice in her state was three years. Consequently, Emily lost her chance to seek legal remedy for her suffering.

Scenario 3: Property Damage Case

Hypothesis: Sarah's property was damaged due to a neighbor's negligence. She tried to settle the matter privately with the neighbor to avoid legal hassles. After one year of back-and-forth discussions, Sarah decided to file a lawsuit. However, the statute of limitations for property damage in her state was one year. Her lawsuit was deemed time-barred, and she couldn't recover the costs for property repair.

In each scenario, the individuals delayed taking legal action for various reasons. Their lack of attention to the statute of limitations resulted in their inability to pursue legal recourse. These examples highlight the importance of being aware of and respecting legal timeframes. Seeking timely legal advice and acting within the statute of limitations is crucial for upholding one's right to seek justice and compensation.

Alright, let's talk about why these things called statutes of limitations are even put in place in the legal world. Imagine you're playing a video game and there's a timer counting down , that's kind of like what a statute of limitations is in real life for legal stuff. So, first off, these rules are there to keep things fair for everyone involved. Let's say something happened, like a car accident or a slip at a store and years later, out of the blue, you decide to sue. By that time, evidence might have gone missing, or people might not remember things clearly. It wouldn't be fair to the person you're suing if they can’t defend themselves properly because too much time has passed. That's where the statute of limitations comes in, it's like saying, “Hey, you’ve got this much time to bring up your lawsuit.”

These rules also give a nudge to people who’ve been hurt or wronged to get moving on their legal claims and not just sit on them. It's like, if you know you've only got a limited time to act, you're probably going to get on it quicker. This helps sort out issues faster instead of letting them drag on forever.

Plus, these time limits help wrap things up and give everyone involved some closure. Nobody wants to be worrying for years that someone might sue them over something that happened a long time ago. It helps people move on, knowing there's an end date to when legal stuff can be brought up.

Now, why is it super important to know about these statutes of limitations? Well, if you don't start your lawsuit within that time frame, you might lose your chance to sue altogether, even if you had a good case. It's like missing the deadline for a big project , once it's passed, there's not much you can do. Knowing the deadline is also key for planning your case. It gives you and your lawyer enough time to gather all your evidence, talk things out with insurance companies, and build a solid case. Plus, it's just peace of mind, right? Knowing there's a clear time frame means you have an idea of when things need to get moving and when they might get sorted out.

In short, the statute of limitations is like a clock ticking on your chance to take legal action. It keeps things fair, encourages you to deal with your legal issues in good time, and helps everyone involved get some closure. So, if something happens and you think you might want to sue, it's pretty important to get clued up on these time limits. It could make all the difference in getting what you're owed or missing out completely.

Now that we've talked about statutes of limitations and why they're like a ticking clock on your ability to bring a lawsuit, let's shift gears a bit and dive into something just as crucial, getting medical care after an accident. See, while keeping an eye on the legal time frame is super important, it's also vital not to lose sight of your health. After all, what's a legal victory if you haven't taken care of yourself first? So, let's chat about why zipping over to a doctor or a hospital ASAP after an accident isn't just good for your recovery but can also be a game-changer for any legal action you might take. Remember, those medical records aren't just papers, they're the story of your injury and healing, and they often speak volumes in a courtroom.

So, let's chat about why getting medical care quickly after an accident is super important, not just for your health but also for any legal stuff you might need to deal with afterward. We'll also talk about your rights as a patient, like picking your own doctors, understanding your treatment options, and keeping your medical info private. First up, why you should hustle to get medical attention after an accident. It's all about catching any injuries early, especially the sneaky ones that don't show up right away, like internal damage or brain stuff. Waiting too long could make things worse or drag out your recovery. Plus, those medical records are super important if you need to prove in court that you got hurt because of the accident.

Now, about choosing your doctors. You totally have the right to pick who treats you. Sure, your insurance might point you towards certain docs, but at the end of the day, it's your call. And if your injuries are kind of specific, you might need to see specialists, like bone doctors or brain doctors. Understanding your treatment is also a big deal. This is where informed consent comes in. It's just a fancy way of saying you should know what's going on with your treatment and what the risks and benefits are. Don't be shy about asking questions. The more you know, the better decisions you can make.

Your medical records are private stuff. Doctors and hospitals have to keep it that way, thanks to the law. If you're dealing with a lawsuit because of your accident, you might need to share these records with your lawyer or the insurance folks, but it's gotta be done the right way. Sometimes, you might not be feeling a particular treatment or procedure, and that's okay. You have the right to say no to any medical treatment. Just make sure you understand what that means for your health. Talking it through with your doctor is always a good idea.

Let's look at some hypothetical scenarios that demonstrate why it's so crucial to seek medical care immediately after an accident:

<u>Scenario 1: Hidden Injuries in a Car Accident</u>

Hypothesis: Mike was involved in a minor car collision. He felt fine right after the accident, just a bit shaken, so he decided not to visit the doctor. Days later, he started experiencing severe headaches and dizziness. It turned out he had a concussion that wasn't immediately apparent. Delaying medical care not only worsened his condition but also made it harder to link his symptoms directly to the accident, complicating his insurance claim.

<u>Scenario 2: Aggravating a Minor Injury</u>

Hypothesis: Sarah twisted her ankle after slipping in a store but brushed it off as a minor sprain and didn't seek immediate medical attention. Over the next week, she continued her regular activities, inadvertently aggravating the injury. What could have been a simple treatment turned into a more complex medical issue requiring surgery, significantly increasing her medical costs and recovery time.

Scenario 3: Impact on Legal Claims

Hypothesis: Alex got injured at work but delayed going to the doctor, hoping the pain would subside. When he finally decided to file a worker's compensation claim, the gap between the accident and the medical visit was questioned by the insurance company. They argued that the injury might not have been work-related, jeopardizing his compensation claim.

Scenario 4: Underestimating Internal Injuries

Hypothesis: After a minor motorcycle accident, James avoided going to the hospital because he only had a few bruises. A few days later, he collapsed due to internal bleeding that had gone unnoticed and untreated. This delay in medical care nearly cost him his life and led to a much longer and more complicated recovery process.

In each of these scenarios, the individuals underestimated their injuries or delayed seeking medical care for various reasons. This delay not only worsened their medical conditions but also affected their insurance and legal processes, showing how immediate medical attention is crucial both for health and for ensuring legal and financial protection following an accident.

Alright, so we've been talking about all the ins and outs of dealing medical care, now, let's dive into something a bit more technical but super important, it's called comparative negligence. This is a big deal in some places and can really change how your case pans out. Let's break it down and see how it can affect everything if you find yourself in an accident.

So, what's this comparative negligence all about? Imagine you're in an accident, and it turns out you're partly to blame for what happened. Maybe you weren't looking where you were going, or perhaps you forgot to signal while driving. In some areas, if you had even a small part in causing the accident, it could seriously reduce or even affect your chances of getting any compensation. It's like if two soccer players go for the ball and both kinda foul each other, it's not just one person's fault.

Now, how does this play out in court or with the insurance companies? Well, if you're trying to get some compensation for your injury, the other side might dig deep to find any bit of evidence that you were partly at fault. They'll go over everything with a fine-tooth comb, the accident details, witness stories, and what you were doing at that time. It's their way of trying to show that you should get less money or maybe even none at all.

This is where having a good lawyer really matters. You need someone who knows their stuff, someone who can gather all the evidence to show that the other party was more at fault. It's all about building a strong case to make sure you're not left holding the bag for something that wasn't totally your fault.

And if you're thinking about settling the case without going to court, knowing about comparative negligence is crucial. Your lawyer might work out a deal that considers the chance that you get less than what you deserve or could end up with nothing. It's a bit of a balancing act, figuring out what's the best move.

In a nutshell, comparative negligence can throw a big wrench in your plans for getting compensation after an accident. It's something you need to be aware of, depending on where you live. Having a clear understanding of how your own actions might impact your case, and having a savvy lawyer, can make a huge difference in how things turn out. It's all about being prepared and knowing the rules of the game.

Let's explore a few hypothetical scenarios to illustrate how comparative negligence can affect a personal injury case:

Scenario 1: Pedestrian Accident

Hypothesis: Emma is walking while texting and steps onto the street without noticing the oncoming traffic. She gets hit by a car and sustains injuries. Emma files a lawsuit against the driver. However, it's established that she wasn't paying attention to traffic signals due to being distracted by her phone. Under comparative negligence laws, her compensation might be significantly reduced or even denied because her own negligence contributed to the accident.

Scenario 2: Car Accident at an Intersection

Hypothesis: Jack runs a red light and collides with another vehicle driven by Lucy, who was speeding. Both sustain injuries and damages to their cars. In a lawsuit, it is found that while Jack was primarily at fault for running the red light, Lucy's speeding contributed to the severity of the accident. Under comparative negligence, Lucy's potential compensation for her injuries and car damage may be reduced due to her part in the accident.

Scenario 3: Slip and Fall in a Store

Hypothesis: Mike slips and falls in a grocery store, injuring his back. He sues the store for negligence because the floor was wet. However, the store presents evidence showing that there were multiple caution signs around the wet area, which Mike ignored because he was browsing on his phone. If the court finds Mike's distraction contributed to the accident, his ability to recover damages might be reduced or even completely barred.

In each of these scenarios, the injured party's own actions contributed to their accidents to varying degrees. In areas where comparative negligence is applied or some principle similar to it, even a small amount of negligence on the part of the plaintiff can lead to a significant reduction or complete denial of compensation. These examples underscore the importance of understanding how your own behavior in an incident can impact your legal rights and the outcomes of a personal injury case.

Finally, a quick heads up about dealing with insurance companies after an accident. They might want you to give a recorded statement about what happened. It's a good idea to chat with a personal injury lawyer before you go down that road. You gotta know your rights and how what you say could affect your case. So, there you have it. Getting medical help fast, knowing your patient rights, and understanding how all this plays into any legal action you might take are key pieces of the puzzle when you're dealing with the fallout from an accident.

Chapter 6:
Choosing the Right Attorney

The journey to recovery after sustaining a personal injury involves often navigating a complex legal landscape, one that can significantly impact your path to healing and justice. Central to this journey is the pivotal decision of choosing the right personal injury lawyer. This choice is more than just picking a legal representative. It is, in fact, about finding an ally who can adeptly guide you through the legal intricacies, advocate for your rights, and strive for the compensation you deserve. In this chapter, we delve into the crucial factors that should guide your selection process, ensuring that you make an informed decision tailored to your specific needs and circumstances.

We will begin by exploring the importance of specialization and experience in personal injury law. Understanding why expertise in this particular field is essential can help you identify a lawyer who is well-equipped to handle the unique challenges of your case. Next, we turn our focus to the lawyer's reputation and track record, discussing how a history of successful outcomes and positive client and peer reviews can be indicative of a lawyer's capability and reliability.

Communication and comfort level with the lawyer form the next critical aspect. The importance of clear, open communication and establishing a comfortable, trusting relationship with your lawyer cannot be overstressed, as these elements are foundational to a successful attorney-client partnership.

The chapter will also cover the practical considerations of a lawyer's resources and availability, highlighting why these factors are key in ensuring your case receives the attention and expertise it requires. Furthermore, we will discuss the often-overlooked details of fee structures and transparency, providing insights into how understanding the financial aspects of legal representation can prevent future misunderstandings and ensure a fair agreement.

Finally, we'll guide you through preparing for and making the most of your initial consultation, including what questions to ask and what information to gather. We'll also touch upon the importance of verifying credentials and checking disciplinary records, ensuring that your chosen lawyer not only meets but exceeds professional standards.

By the end of this chapter, you will be equipped with the knowledge and insights necessary to confidently choose a personal injury lawyer who not only understands the legalities of your case but also aligns with your personal values and expectations, setting a foundation for a successful legal journey.

Experience and qualifications matter, but you also have to justify the cost. There are attorneys who will not charge you if you lose the case. However, some may charge by the hour. The first thing you must do is to relax and take a deep breath. It may sound complex, but we live in a time where every piece of information is at our fingertips.

Alright, let's chat about why it's really important to have a lawyer who knows their stuff when it comes to personal injury law. Think of it like needing a specialist doctor for a specific health issue. You wouldn't go to an eye doctor for a broken leg, right? In the same way, for personal injury cases, whether it's a car wreck, a slip at the store, or a botched medical procedure, having a lawyer who's an expert in personal injury law is crucial. They've got all the know-how about the rules and tricks of the trade to handle your unique situation.

Now, experience counts for a lot here. Say you've got a lawyer who's dealt with a ton of cases like yours. They're going to know exactly what moves to make. For example, if you've had a nasty fall, a lawyer who's done plenty of slip-and-fall cases will know all the common excuses property owners use and how to knock those defenses down. Their past successes, or even the times they didn't win, teach them valuable lessons that they can apply to your case.

But it's not just about their track record in court. You'll want to hear from people they've helped before. What do their clients say about them? Are other lawyers giving them a thumbs up? This kind of feedback can give you a good idea of whether they're the right fit for you.

Communication’s a big deal, too. You need someone who’s going to keep you in the loop, explain all the legal jargon in plain English, and actually answer when you call or email them. And it's got to be someone you feel comfortable with. Dealing with legal stuff can be stressful, so having a lawyer who makes you feel at ease can make a world of difference. Let's talk about their resources and time, as well. The right lawyer should have the manpower, the experts, and the tech to really dig into your case. Plus, they should be able to give your case the attention it deserves. If they're juggling too many cases at once, yours might not get the focus it needs.

Now, about the money side of things. Many personal injury lawyers work on what’s called a contingency fee basis. This means they only get paid if you win your case. It's important to understand how this works and what percentage they’ll take. Also, be clear about any extra costs that might pop up, like court fees or charges for getting medical records.

When you first meet with a lawyer, it’s your chance to grill them a bit. Ask about their experience, how they plan to tackle your case, and how they’ve handled similar cases in the past. See how they respond. Do they have a clear plan? Do they seem like they know what they’re talking about? This is also when you figure out if their style works for you.

Checking their credentials is key, too. Make sure they’re actually licensed to practice in your area and haven’t had any major issues with the law themselves. You can usually find this info on the state bar association's website or their professional profiles.

So, picking the right lawyer for a personal injury case? It's a big decision. You want someone with the right knowledge, a solid track record, and a style that meshes with yours. It's about finding someone you trust to take on your case and really go to bat for you. Choose wisely, and it can make all the difference in getting the outcome you deserve.

Let's explore a few hypothetical scenarios that highlight the potential consequences of choosing the wrong attorney for a personal injury case:

Scenario 1: Lack of Specialized Knowledge

Hypothesis: Bob chose a family friend as his attorney for a complex medical malpractice case because of their long-standing relationship. However, the attorney primarily practiced corporate law and had little experience with medical malpractice. As a result, they missed critical nuances in medical regulations and failed to consult appropriate medical experts, leading to Bob's case being dismissed due to insufficient evidence.

Scenario 2: Overwhelmed by Caseload

Hypothesis: Sarah hired a personal injury lawyer based on a flashy advertisement. However, this lawyer was handling too many cases simultaneously and couldn't dedicate enough time to Sarah's case.

Important deadlines were missed, and Sarah felt her case wasn't given the attention it required. Consequently, Sarah settled for a much lower compensation than she could have potentially received with a more attentive lawyer.

Scenario 3: Poor Communication and Lack of Transparency

Hypothesis: After an auto accident, Carlos hired an attorney who seemed confident and assertive. However, as the case progressed, Carlos found it difficult to get updates. The attorney was often unavailable and unclear about the case's status and potential outcomes. This lack of communication led to Carlos feeling out of the loop and unprepared for the eventual settlement negotiation, resulting in him agreeing to terms that were not in his best interest.

Scenario 4: Inexperienced in Negotiations

Hypothesis: Jenna hired a lawyer who was a recent law school graduate. While enthusiastic, the lawyer lacked experience in negotiating with insurance companies. During negotiations, the lawyer was easily outmaneuvered by the experienced insurance adjusters, leading to a settlement far below what Jenna's case was worth, and not covering all her medical expenses and lost wages.

Scenario 5: Ethical Concerns and Reputation

Hypothesis: Derek chose a lawyer known for aggressive tactics and a 'win-at-all-costs' mentality. As the case unfolded, it became apparent that the lawyer was willing to bend ethical rules to gain an advantage. This not only made Derek uncomfortable but also ended up harming his case when the lawyer's reputation and tactics were frowned upon by the judge, negatively impacting the case's credibility.

In each scenario, the choice of an inappropriate attorney for various reasons, lack of specialization, overwhelming caseload, poor communication, inexperience in negotiations, or ethical concerns, had detrimental effects on the outcome of the case. These examples underscore the importance of carefully selecting an attorney who is not only specialized in personal injury law but also has the appropriate experience, capacity, communication skills, and ethical standards to effectively handle your case.

Chapter 7: The Legal Process Demystified

Stepping into the world of civil lawsuits can often feel like navigating through a dense, unfamiliar forest, especially if you're grappling with the aftermath of an event like a personal injury. From the pivotal initial consultation with an attorney to the intricacies of prelitigation negotiations, we'll walk you through each step in a way that's conversational and easy to grasp. Think of this as a friendly chat about the legal landscape, aimed at demystifying the process and empowering you with the knowledge to navigate it confidently.

Let's imagine you're Alex, who recently got into a car accident. It's not the stuff of storybooks, but it has left you with a broken arm and a stack of bills that seem to grow taller by the day. Frustrated and unsure, you think, "Maybe I should get some legal advice." This is where the journey into the world of personal injury begins.

So, you find yourself in the office of a lawyer named DiBella, ready to unravel your tale. This first meeting, the initial consultation, is pretty crucial. It's where you lay all your cards on the table. You tell DiBella about the accident, where it happened, how it all went down, and how you ended up with the injuries.

DiBella, with a knack for details, listens to every word. They occasionally stop you to look at the medical records you've brought along, the photos of your damaged car, and even the emails you've exchanged with the insurance company. DiBella's trying to piece together your story, asking about any past injuries or legal issues you've had. It's all about seeing the full picture, figuring out if you've got a solid case to bring to the courtroom.

Then comes the part where DiBella talks strategy. It's not like they're revealing a secret battle plan, but more giving you a sense of the direction they might take with your case. They explain how the law sees situations like yours and what your options might be.

One important thing that comes up is the fee structure. In personal injury cases like yours, lawyers like DiBella often work on a contingency fee basis. This means they get paid a portion of whatever money you might win in your case. It's like they're invested in your success.

You're not just nodding along, you're also firing off questions. "Have you handled cases like mine before? Who exactly will be working on my case? How long do you think this will all take?" You want to know how DiBella communicates with clients and what kind of outcomes they've seen in similar cases.

This first meeting is more than just an exchange of information, it's setting the stage for what's to come. It's your chance to feel out DiBella as your potential legal champion and for DiBella to see if your case is one they can win. Walking out of DiBella's office, you feel a mix of nerves and relief. The legal world isn’t as intimidating as it seemed, and you're one step closer to finding your way through this maze.

What happens after the initial consultation? Let's talk about what happens before you might end up in court for a personal injury case. This is the phase where you try to work things out with the insurance company of the person or entity that caused your injury. It's called prelitigation negotiation, and it's a pretty big deal because it can mean settling things without having to go through the whole courtroom drama.

Now, the first thing you gotta do is get your ducks in a row, evidence-wise. Think of it as gathering your arsenal for the negotiation battle. You need to collect all your medical records that show what injuries you got, the treatments you’ve had, and what you might need down the line. This isn't just about now, it's about how this injury could affect you in the future too.

Next up, you need to show what happened during the accident. This means pulling together the police report if there is one, photos of the accident scene, any statements from people who saw it happen, and anything else that paints a picture of how the accident went down.

Don’t forget about the money part. If you've lost money because you couldn't work due to your injury, you need to show that. Gather stuff like your pay stubs or letters from your employer that spell out what income you missed out on.

Now, when it comes to figuring out what you should get from the insurance company, there are two main types of damages. First, there are economic damages, these are the ones you can put a clear dollar amount on, like your medical bills, the wages you lost, and any other expenses you had because of the injury. Then, there are non-economic damages. These are a bit trickier because they're not about direct costs. They're about the less tangible stuff like the pain and suffering you went through, any emotional stress, and how this injury might have stopped you from enjoying your life like you used to.

This whole negotiation dance is about getting a settlement that's fair and covers all these bases. It's a bit of give and take, but the goal is to reach an agreement that compensates you for what you've been through, without having to step foot in a courtroom.

It's time to enter the next critical phase, the demand process. This is where the chess game really begins. You're moving from gathering your arsenal to actually laying out your battle strategy. The demand letter is your first major play, a document that not only puts forth your case in a formal, structured manner but also sets the tone for the negotiations to come. It's like stepping up to the negotiation table, laying your cards out, and waiting to see the insurance company's response. So, let's delve into what crafting an effective demand letter entails and how it can pave the way toward a successful settlement.

It's like the opening move in a chess game, and it's pretty important for setting the tone of your negotiations with the insurance company. Think of the demand letter as your official way of saying, "Hey, you owe me for what happened." It's your first step in formally telling the insurance company about your injury and what you expect them to pay. It's like laying your cards on the table and saying, "This is what I've been through, and here's what I think is fair."

Imagine you're telling a story. You start with what happened, where, when, and how the injury occurred. Be detailed because this sets the scene. Then, you move on to describe your injuries and the kind of medical treatment you've had to endure. This isn't just a list, it's about painting a picture of your pain and suffering.

Next, you talk money. You list out all your expenses, the medical bills, any therapy you've had, the wages you lost because you couldn't work, and so on. But it's not all just about bills and lost paychecks. You also talk about the pain and emotional stress, the stuff that doesn't have a price tag but definitely counts.

Then, you need to explain why the other party is at fault. It's like connecting the dots between their actions (or lack thereof) and your injury. Finally, you put a number on it, the amount you're asking for. This number's usually a bit higher than what you're hoping to get, kind of leaving room to negotiate. Don't forget to attach all the evidence you've got medical records, bills, maybe even a note from your boss about the work you missed.

Once you send this letter, it's over to the insurance company. They might agree to your terms (ideal, but not super common), flat out reject your claim (not great), or more likely, come back with a counteroffer. This is usually lower than what you've asked for.

Now comes the back-and-forth. It's like haggling at a market. Your lawyer will be doing most of the talking here, using their skills to argue why you deserve more. They'll help you weigh the offers, looking at the strengths and weaknesses of your case.

If you and the insurance company manage to find middle ground, great! You'll get the terms written up, which usually includes a part where you agree not to sue them in the future for this injury. Once you sign off, the insurance company will process your payment. But what if you can't reach an agreement? Well, then you might be looking at taking your case to court. It's like deciding whether to keep haggling or just walk away and try a different approach.

So, that's the gist of it. The demand letter is your opening statement in this negotiation process, setting the stage for what's to come. It's a mix of storytelling, fact-presenting, and a bit of strategic thinking, all rolled into one.

After the back-and-forth of prelitigation negotiations, let's say you and the insurance company just can't see eye to eye. You've had your talks, sent your demand letter, but the settlement you need isn't coming through. This is where you and your attorney might have a serious chat about shifting gears and heading to court. Filing a lawsuit is a big decision, and it's not just about being right or wrong. It's a move that requires careful thought about what you stand to gain versus what it might cost you in time, money, and stress.

When you're tangled up in a personal injury case, one big question often pops up, should you settle the case before it ever gets to court, in what we call the prelitigation phase? It's like standing at a crossroads and trying to figure out which path to take. Let's chat about the pros and cons of settling early.

First off, settling early can be a huge time-saver. Court cases can drag on for what feels like forever. Settling early is like taking a shortcut to the end of the journey. It's quicker, and you can move on with your life. Then there's the cost aspect. Going to court can be really expensive. Lawyers' fees, court costs, and all that. Settling early often means you spend less money. It's like opting for a budget-friendly route instead of a pricey, scenic one. Another big plus is certainty. When you settle, you know exactly what you're getting. It's a sure thing, like booking a guaranteed seat on a flight instead of hoping for an upgrade. In court, you never really know how things will turn out. It's a gamble. Also, settling is private. Court cases can get public, airing your personal stuff for all to see. Settling keeps it all under wraps, like a quiet, behind-the-scenes deal.

On the flip side, sometimes settling early means you might get less money than you could have if you'd gone to court. It's like selling your old phone quickly at a lower price instead of waiting to find a buyer who might pay more. Settling also means you might not get your "day in court." For some people, having their story heard and validated in front of a judge or jury is really important. Settling skips that part. It's like missing out on the chance to tell your side of the story at a big family gathering. And let's not forget, when you settle, the other side doesn't have to admit they were wrong. If getting that admission is important to you, settling might feel a bit unsatisfying.

So, What's the Best Move? Deciding whether to settle or go to court is a bit like choosing between a guaranteed, but maybe smaller, prize now or a chance at the jackpot later with no guarantees. It depends on what matters most to you, speed, cost, certainty, privacy, or maybe the principle of the thing. It's a personal choice, and it's always smart to chat it through with your lawyer to make sure you're making the best decision for your situation.

Chapter 8:
When to Consider Filing a Lawsuit

In life, unforeseen events can unravel the sense of order and security we cherish. Among these, personal injuries arising from countless circumstances stand out as profoundly disruptive, often leaving trails of physical, emotional, and financial upheaval. As you navigate these turbulent waters, the question of whether to pursue legal action looms large.

This book is not just about legal processes. It's about understanding when stepping into a courtroom becomes a necessary part of the process of resolving a legal matter. Whether it's a slip on an unmarked wet floor, a harrowing accident on the highway, or harm due to medical negligence, each situation carries its unique set of challenges and considerations.

For many, the idea of a lawsuit is daunting. Images of courtrooms, legal jargon, and the unpredictability of outcomes may cloud judgment. This book aims to demystify the process, offering insight into how the legal system can work for you and when it is wise to harness its power in pursuit of justice.

Remember that each case, like each individual, is unique. There is no one-size-fits-all answer to the question of pursuing a lawsuit. However, armed with knowledge, guided by wisdom, and supported by expertise, you can make an informed decision that aligns with your quest for justice and personal recovery, you decide to file a lawsuit.

But before you get too deep into this, you and your lawyer should sit down and really weigh the odds. They'll talk you through what to expect, how strong your case is, and what it's going to cost, both in dollars and in your personal time. For instance, you might need to take time off work for depositions or to gather more information. It's not just a legal commitment but a personal one too.

Starting a lawsuit begins with the drafting of a civil cmplaint. Once your complaint is ready, it gets filed in court. The court needs to be the right one. One that actually has the power to decide your case. And yes, there are fees involved when you file. Then, there's the task of officially letting the other party know they're being sued, which is called "service of process." Getting this step right is crucial, mess it up, and your case could be delayed or even thrown out.

Once the other party, now the defendant, gets your complaint, they have a set amount of time to respond. They can agree with what you say (not likely), flat-out deny it, or throw in some legal defenses. Then you enter the discovery phase. This is where both sides start digging for more information. You'll be swapping documents, asking each other questions in writing, and sometimes sitting down for depositions, where you're asked questions under oath. It's like putting all the puzzle pieces on the table to see what the full picture really is.

During all this, there might be motions filed, requests to the court to make decisions about certain aspects of your case. Maybe one side wants to dismiss part of the case, or maybe they think the whole thing can be decided without a trial. And there's always a chance for mediation, where a neutral person tries to help both sides come to an agreement. It's a less formal, often less stressful way to maybe settle things without a full trial.

If none of this leads to a settlement, then you're heading to trial. Preparing for trial is a big job. You and your lawyer will go over your evidence, prepare witnesses, and fine-tune your legal arguments. You might even do practice runs, called mock trials, to get ready.

Choosing to go to trial isn't just about proving you're right. It's a gamble. Trials are unpredictable, you never know how a jury might see things. They can also take a long time and cost more than settling out of court. And it's not just a legal fight, it can be an emotional one too, with your personal life on display in a public courtroom.

Then, there's the chance the other side might appeal if they lose, dragging the whole thing out even longer. And if the defendant goes bankrupt during this process, that opens up a whole new can of worms. You might end up getting less than you hoped for, or even nothing at all.

Remember, even when a trial is looming, the door to settlement is still open. Sometimes, just the pressure of an upcoming trial can get both sides talking settlement again. So, as you can see, deciding to go to trial in a personal injury case is no simple choice. It's a road that requires careful navigation, a solid understanding of what's at stake, and a willingness to see it through, come what may.

Navigating the legal landscape of a personal injury lawsuit can be a defining journey for anyone. This section delves into the significant legal implications of bringing such a case to court. We explore the critical process of establishing liability, the potential of setting legal precedents, and the public nature of court records. Understanding the legal impacts provided below is essential for anyone preparing to step into the legal arena as they shape the course and consequences of the lawsuit.

So, when you're thinking about taking your personal injury case to court, it's a bit like deciding to climb a mountain. You know it's going to be a tough journey, but you're hoping the view from the top is worth it. Let's break down what this climb involves, from figuring out who's to blame to the potential payout and everything in between.

First things first, establishing who's responsible, legally speaking, is a huge deal. It's not just about who pays up in the end. It also shapes how insurance companies and everyone else sees the whole situation. And let's not forget, people are watching what happens in your case might sway public opinion or even set a precedent for future cases. Kind of like being the first person to carve a new path up that mountain.

Now, onto the money talk. Winning a lawsuit could mean a nice financial cushion, especially if you're dealing with long-term injuries or can't work like you used to. But don't forget, climbing this legal mountain isn't cheap. You've got lawyer fees, court costs, and all that jazz. And even if you win big, it might take a while before you see any of that cash.

But it's not all about dollars and cents. Going to court can be an emotional rollercoaster. You might feel stressed out, and it could strain your relationships. On the flip side, getting that legal stamp of approval that you were wronged and deserve compensation, can bring a sense of closure.

Let's talk about time. Court cases can drag on... and on. It's not just the days you spend in court, it's all the prep work, meetings with your lawyer, and endless waiting for the next step. Your daily life could be turned upside down, and those hobbies or hangouts with friends might have to take a backseat.

Then there's the social side of things. Being involved in a lawsuit might change how people see you, in your neighborhood, at work, or even among your friends. And if you're working, juggling the case with your job can be tricky, especially if your injury's affecting your work performance.

Amid all this, it's easy to forget about the most important thing, your health. Focusing so much on the legal battle might mean putting your recovery on the back burner. It's crucial to keep an eye on your well-being, both physically and mentally. Now, just when you think you've got it all figured out, life throws a curveball. Maybe the person you're suing has a change of fortune, like going bankrupt, which could toss your whole case into limbo. Or a new witness pops up, changing the whole game.

Remember, a lot of what happens in court is out of your hands. The judge and jury call the shots, and their decisions can be pretty unpredictable. Plus, the court's schedule isn't always set in stone, so you might find yourself playing the waiting game more often than you'd like.

So, What's the Bottom Line? Deciding to sue isn't a decision to make lightly. It's like choosing to climb that mountain knowing the risks, the costs, and the time it'll take. But if you reach the top, the rewards can be life-changing. Just make sure you have a good guide (your lawyer) and you're prepared for the journey ahead.

In conclusion, there are some good reasons to take the plunge, but there are also a few things that might make you want to sit on the edge a little longer. Let's start on a positive note. Filing a lawsuit could mean you get the compensation you deserve. Think about it like finally getting a long-overdue bill paid. This could cover everything from medical bills to lost wages, and it can be a huge relief, especially if you're struggling financially because of your injury. Another good thing is the sense of justice it can bring. If you've been wronged, there's something deeply satisfying about having your day in court, telling your story, and hearing a judge or jury say, "You're right, and you deserve to be compensated." It's a bit like getting an official stamp of validation on your experience.

Now, for the not-so-great parts. Lawsuits can be like marathons, long, exhausting, and sometimes with an uncertain finish line. It's not just about the time in court. There's preparation, meetings, and a lot of waiting around for the next step. If you're not the patient type, this can be pretty frustrating. And let's talk about the cost. Legal battles can be expensive, even with a lawyer working on contingency (where they only get paid if you win). If things don't go your way, you could end up with a lighter wallet and nothing to show for it. The stress and emotional toll are also worth considering. It's not just a legal process, it's a personal journey. The ups and downs of a lawsuit can take a lot out of you, not just mentally, but it can strain your relationships and impact your everyday life. With lawsuits, nothing is a sure bet. Even with a strong case, the outcome can be unpredictable. Juries can be fickle, and laws can be interpreted in different ways. You might go in thinking you have a winning hand, only to be surprised by the verdict.

Deciding to file a lawsuit is a big decision. It's not just about whether you're right or wrong, but it's also about weighing the potential benefits against the time, money, and emotional energy you'll have to invest. It's like weighing whether that jump into the pool is worth the potential shock of the cold water. The best approach? Talk it through with a good lawyer, consider your options, and then make the call that feels right for you.

Chapter 9:
Emotional and Psychological Aspects of a Lawsuit

Mental health plays a crucial role in the realm of lawsuits, especially in cases related to personal injury. Its impact is twofold, firstly, as a significant component of damages in legal claims, and secondly, as a consequence of the litigation process itself.

In personal injury cases, it's not uncommon for plaintiffs to suffer from psychological injuries alongside physical ones. These can include conditions like post-traumatic stress disorder (PTSD), anxiety, and depression, which stem directly from the traumatic incident. The mental health impact is a key aspect of the damages claimed. It falls under the category of 'pain and suffering' and involves assessing the emotional distress caused by the incident, which can significantly affect the individual's quality of life. Expert testimony from mental health professionals often plays a vital role in these cases, helping to establish the extent of psychological harm.

The mental health implications of being involved in a lawsuit itself are also noteworthy. Litigation can be an inherently stressful experience characterized by uncertainty and the adversarial nature of legal proceedings. This environment can exacerbate existing mental health conditions or even trigger new ones. For many plaintiffs, particularly in personal injury cases, the process of discussing and reliving the traumatic events during the litigation can be retraumatizing. The prolonged nature of many legal battles only adds to this stress, contributing to a sustained period of anxiety and uncertainty.

Moreover, individuals involved in lawsuits, especially high-profile cases, might experience feelings of isolation or stigma. This emotional toll is not always acknowledged, but it can profoundly affect an individual's well-being and their day-to-day life.

It's essential for individuals involved in lawsuits to have not only skilled legal representation but also access to mental health support to mitigate these challenges. Lawyers play a critical role in managing the stressors of litigation by effectively handling the legal processes and maintaining clear and supportive communication with their clients. Concurrently, psychological counseling or therapy can be invaluable for individuals coping with the mental health impacts of both their original trauma and the stress of the legal proceedings.

The intersection of mental health and lawsuits is complex and significant. Acknowledging and addressing the mental health aspects in legal claims and throughout the litigation process is essential for the holistic resolution of these cases and the well-being of those involved.

Coping with stress and anxiety requires a multifaceted approach, focusing on both mental and physical well-being.

Recognizing and accepting your feelings is a crucial first step. It's normal to feel stressed or anxious in challenging situations, and acknowledging these emotions is key to dealing with them effectively.

One of the most beneficial strategies is to establish a strong support system. Friends, family, or support groups can provide invaluable assistance. Simply talking about your worries and stresses with someone who understands can make a significant difference in how you feel.

Additionally, practicing relaxation techniques can be highly effective. Techniques like deep breathing exercises, meditation, or yoga can help calm your mind and reduce anxiety levels. Incorporating these practices into your daily routine can provide both immediate relief and long-term benefits.

Regular physical activity is another important aspect of managing stress and anxiety. Exercise releases endorphins, chemicals in your brain that act as natural painkillers and mood elevators. Even a daily walk, jog, or a session of light exercise can contribute to improved mental health.

Maintaining a healthy diet also plays a role. A well-balanced diet, rich in fruits, vegetables, and whole grains, can help regulate your mood and energy levels. Avoiding excessive caffeine and sugar can prevent spikes and crashes in energy that can exacerbate stress and anxiety.

Setting aside time for hobbies and activities you enjoy is also crucial. Engaging in activities that distract you from your worries and provide a sense of satisfaction can be very therapeutic. Whether it's reading, gardening, painting, or any other hobby, dedicating time to it can offer a much-needed break from stress.

Mindfulness and grounding techniques can help keep you connected to the present moment and ward off anxious thoughts about the future. Practices like mindful breathing, focusing on your senses, or mindful observation can be integrated into daily life and help manage anxiety spikes.

Lastly, don't hesitate to seek professional help if stress and anxiety become overwhelming. A mental health professional can provide tailored strategies to cope with anxiety, offer support, and, if necessary, recommend medication or other treatments. Remember, seeking help is a sign of strength, not weakness, and it's a crucial step towards taking control of your mental health.

Seeking support through therapy and support groups is an essential aspect of managing stress, anxiety, or dealing with the aftermath of traumatic experiences. These resources offer a safe space to explore feelings, develop coping strategies, and connect with others facing similar challenges.

Therapy, especially with a qualified mental health professional, can be incredibly beneficial. A therapist can provide a non-judgmental, confidential environment where you can express and work through your emotions. Various forms of therapy, including cognitive-behavioral therapy (CBT), psychotherapy, or counseling, can help in addressing the root causes of stress and anxiety. Therapists can equip you with practical tools and techniques to manage your symptoms, improve your emotional resilience, and enhance your overall mental well-being.

Support groups, on the other hand, offer the unique advantage of shared experiences. They bring together individuals who are going through similar situations, providing a sense of community and mutual understanding. In these groups, members often find comfort and encouragement in knowing they are not alone in their struggles. Support groups can be particularly helpful in providing peer support, sharing coping strategies, and offering practical advice based on real-life experiences.

Whether it's through one-on-one therapy sessions or group meetings, seeking professional and communal support can play a vital role in your journey toward healing and mental wellness. These avenues of support encourage openness and vulnerability in a structured, supportive environment, fostering a path to recovery and empowerment.

Managing expectations in a lawsuit is crucial for several reasons. It helps maintain a realistic perspective on potential outcomes and can reduce additional stress and disappointment. Lawsuits, especially personal injury cases, often come with uncertainties and complexities that can affect the final outcome.

Firstly, understanding the legal process is key. Lawsuits can be lengthy, and the pace of legal proceedings often surprises those unfamiliar with the system. Delays are common, and patience is essential. Recognizing that the wheels of justice turn slowly helps in setting realistic timelines.

It's also important to have realistic expectations regarding the settlement or verdict. While it's natural to hope for the best possible outcome, the reality is that compromises are often necessary. Factors such as the strength of evidence, the clarity of liability, and insurance limits play significant roles in determining settlement amounts. Your attorney can provide guidance on what constitutes a fair and realistic settlement in your case.

Another aspect to manage is the expectation of emotional closure. While a lawsuit can provide financial compensation for damages, it doesn't always equate to emotional closure or justice in the way you might expect. The end of a lawsuit might bring relief, but it's often just one part of a larger healing process, especially in cases of personal injury.

Communication with your attorney is paramount. A good attorney will keep you informed about the progress of your case and help set realistic expectations for outcomes, timelines, and potential hurdles. They should also explain the legal terms and processes in a way that you understand, which can significantly help in managing your expectations.

Finally, prepare for the possibility of an appeal. Even after a verdict is reached, the case might not be over. The losing party may decide to appeal the decision, which can prolong the resolution and impact the final outcome.

In summary, managing expectations in a lawsuit involves understanding the legal process, maintaining realistic perspectives on potential outcomes, and staying informed and patient throughout the journey. Recognizing that a lawsuit is just one step in a broader personal and legal journey can help in maintaining a balanced outlook.

Chapter 10:

Chapter: Navigating the Aftermath of Victory – The Journey Beyond the Courtroom

So, you've just heard the words you've been waiting for: "We find in favor of the plaintiff." Congratulations! Winning your personal injury case is a momentous achievement. It's like reaching the peak of a mountain after a long, arduous climb. But, as with any summit, the journey doesn't end there. Let's talk about what comes next.

Winning the case is one thing, but getting the money? That's a whole new adventure. Imagine it as a treasure hunt. Sometimes, the defendant willingly pays up, which is like finding the treasure chest right under the 'X' on the map. But other times, especially if the defendant is reluctant or unable to pay, you might need to take additional legal steps. This could mean garnishing wages, putting a lien on property, or other legal maneuvers. It's like having to solve a few more riddles before you can claim your prize. Remember, persistence is key. It's normal to feel a bit impatient, but just like any good treasure hunt, it's the persistence and clever strategies that eventually lead to success.

Now, let's talk taxes. Not the most exciting part of your victory, but crucial. Think of it as passing through a toll gate on your way home with your treasure. The good news is, in many places, personal injury settlements aren't taxable, however you should consult a tax professional. However, there are exceptions, like if you're awarded punitive damages or if your settlement includes compensation for lost wages.

It's a good idea to talk to a tax advisor. Understanding your tax obligations ensures you don't get any unpleasant surprises down the road. Think of them as your navigator, helping you safely bring your treasure home without losing any to unforeseen tax traps.

If your injury is long-term or permanent, part of your settlement might be earmarked for future medical costs. This is where careful planning really pays off. It's like charting a course for a long sea voyage. You need to make sure you have enough supplies (funds) to last the entire journey (your lifetime). Accurately calculating these costs can be complex. It involves considering future medical care, potential complications, inflation, and more. It's essential to work with professionals, medical experts, financial planners, to map out this part of your journey accurately. They're like your crew, ensuring that your ship is well-stocked and ready to face whatever the seas might hold.

Winning your case is more than just a legal victory, it's an emotional one too. It's a validation of your struggle, your pain, and your resilience. Let this victory be a reminder of your strength.

Chapter 11:
Outcomes and Moving Forward

The conclusion of a lawsuit, regardless of the outcome, can bring a range of emotions. Relief is common, particularly if the process is lengthy and stressful. However, it's also normal to feel a sense of emptiness or uncertainty about what comes next. If the outcome isn't favorable, feelings of disappointment or frustration may be predominant.

Financially, you may need to adjust to the reality of the settlement or judgment. If you received compensation, planning how to use it effectively, possibly with the help of a financial advisor, is important. This might involve paying off medical debts, planning for future care needs, or rebuilding any financial loss endured due to the dispute. If the outcome isn't financially favorable, you might need to reassess your financial plans and make adjustments accordingly.

Emotionally and psychologically, it's crucial to acknowledge the impact the lawsuit may have had on your life. Stress, anxiety, and the toll of a prolonged legal battle can linger. Seeking support from mental health professionals, engaging in stress-reduction activities, and allowing yourself time to heal are important steps. Engaging in hobbies, reconnecting with friends and family, and returning to normal routines can aid in this recovery process.

If the lawsuit involved personal relationships, rebuilding or redefining these relationships might be necessary. This can be challenging and may require patience, communication, and possibly the help of a mediator or counselor. Finally, reflecting on what you've learned from the experience can be valuable. Many people find that going through a lawsuit provides new insights into their resilience, their values, and their capabilities. It can also offer lessons about the legal system, personal rights, and self-advocacy.

The reality that most cases settle before reaching trial is a significant aspect of the legal landscape, particularly in the realm of civil litigation, including personal injury cases. This trend is driven by several practical and strategic considerations that both plaintiffs and defendants weigh. Firstly, litigation is inherently uncertain. Going to trial means placing the outcome in the hands of a judge or jury, and no matter how strong a case may seem, there's always an element of unpredictability. Both sides face the risk of losing at trial, which can be a strong motivator to find a mutually agreeable solution through settlement.

Settlements also offer more control over the outcome for both parties. Unlike a trial verdict, which is determined by the court, a settlement is a negotiated agreement where both parties have a say. This allows for more tailored solutions and can ensure that the specific needs or concerns of each party are addressed. Financial considerations are another driving factor. Trials are expensive, time-consuming, and resource-intensive. Legal fees, court costs, and other related expenses can accumulate quickly, and for many, this financial burden is a significant deterrent. Settling a case earlier can often be more cost-effective, even if the settlement amount is less than what might be awarded at trial.

The time factor is also crucial. Trials can extend over months or even years, and for many plaintiffs, especially those dealing with injuries or financial hardships, this prolonged process can be untenable. A settlement provides a quicker resolution, allowing them to move forward and focus on recovery or other personal matters. Moreover, trials are public, and for parties interested in maintaining privacy, particularly in sensitive or high-profile cases, the confidentiality of a settlement is appealing. Settlements can be structured to include non-disclosure agreements, keeping the details and often the existence of the settlement private.

Lastly, the emotional and psychological toll of a trial should not be underestimated. The adversarial nature of a trial, the stress of public scrutiny, and the emotional strain of reliving traumatic events can be overwhelming. Settlements can minimize this emotional burden by providing a less confrontational and more predictable path to resolution.

While trials are an important aspect of the legal system, the reality is that the majority of cases settle outside of court. This trend reflects a pragmatic approach to dispute resolution, balancing the risks and costs of litigation with the benefits of a negotiated agreement that serves the interests of all parties involved.

According to Forbes Advisor (Johnson, 2022):

"Personal injury lawsuits almost always end in settlements. According to the U.S. Department of Justice, only 4% to 5% of personal injury cases go all the way to trial.

A study conducted by the Bureau of Justice Statistics in 2005 found that:

- Of all the personal injury cases that went all the way to verdict, the success rate for plaintiffs was about 50%;
- The highest success rate was in auto accident cases, at 61%;
- Plaintiffs were only successful in 19% of medical malpractice trials.

What this means for someone considering a settlement offer is that if you accept the settlement offer, you are 100% guaranteed to get the amount being offered. If you reject it, statistically speaking, your chances are about 50/50. You could end up with an amount greater than the settlement or even end up with nothing.

Of course, there's another possible outcome besides settling or reaching a verdict. Cases can be dismissed at any time and for a variety of reasons. The plaintiff can simply drop the case, but the judge can also dismiss either based on motions of the parties, basically, one side or the other asks the judge to dismiss, or sua sponte (on the court's own accord)." [2]

As you can see from the statistics, most personal injury cases are settled out of court. However, there are cases when a trial is required, and we discussed these situations earlier.

The Forbes article (Johnson, 2022) further states:

> "Compensation in personal injury cases is based on the facts of each case. Compensation is based on the amount of damages caused, or at least it's supposed to be. This makes it difficult to estimate a typical amount of compensation, even for cases of the same type."

---

[2] Johnson, J., JD. (2022, September 22). Personal Injury Settlement Amounts Examples (2023 Guide). *Forbes Advisor.* https://www.forbes.com/advisor/legal/personal-injury/personal-injury-settlement-amounts/

Appealing a Decision

Appealing a decision in a civil lawsuit is a critical process that comes into play when a party is dissatisfied with the court's verdict. It's a complex procedure that involves several steps and considerations.

When a party decides to appeal a court decision, they are essentially asking a higher court to review the trial court's decision for legal errors. The appeal is not about rehashing the facts or evidence of the case but rather about examining whether the law was applied correctly or if legal procedures were properly followed.

The first step in appealing a decision is to file a notice of appeal. This must be done within a prescribed time frame after the judgment in that jurisdiction. Missing this deadline can result in the loss of the right to appeal. The notice of appeal is a formal declaration to the court and the opposing party that you intend to challenge the trial court's decision.

Once the appeal is filed, the appellant (the party appealing the decision) must prepare a legal brief. This document outlines the legal arguments for why the trial court's decision was incorrect. It should reference specific points in the trial record where it is believed the court made errors. The appellee (the party defending the trial court's decision) will also submit a brief countering the appellant's arguments.

In many cases, the appellate court will hold an oral argument, where lawyers from both sides present their cases and answer judges' questions. This is not a presentation of the entire case but rather a focused discussion on specific legal issues.

The appellate court will then review the trial record, the briefs, and the arguments presented. The judges will determine if there were significant legal errors in the trial process that could have affected the outcome. If such errors are found, the appellate court may reverse the trial court's decision, potentially leading to a new trial. Alternatively, the court can affirm the original decision if it finds no substantial errors.

It's important to note that the appeal process can be lengthy and expensive. Moreover, not every case is eligible for appeal, and not all appeals result in the reversal of a decision. The appellate court gives deference to the trial court's findings, particularly regarding the facts of the case, and overturns decisions only when legal errors are clear and significant.

The decision to appeal should be made after careful consideration and consultation with legal counsel, who can assess the likelihood of success and advise on the best course of action. Appeals require a deep understanding of legal principles and appellate procedure, making experienced legal representation crucial in this phase.

Healing and recovery, particularly after a traumatic event or a challenging period such as a lawsuit, are deeply personal and multifaceted processes. They encompass physical, emotional, and often spiritual aspects and can significantly vary from one individual to another. For many, spiritual or philosophical reflection can offer solace and a sense of peace. Whether it's through organized religion, personal spirituality, or philosophical exploration, finding meaning and perspective in the face of adversity can be a powerful component of the healing journey.

It's also important to set realistic expectations for the recovery process. Healing takes time, and it's often non-linear. There may be setbacks or days when emotions feel overwhelming. Recognizing this as a normal part of healing can prevent feelings of frustration or despair.

Lastly, finding a way to express what has been experienced can be cathartic. For some, this might mean talking about their experiences, while for others, it could involve creative expression like writing, painting, or music. Sharing your story when you're ready can not only aid in your own healing but also support others who may be going through similar challenges.

In conclusion, healing and recovery are deeply personal journeys that encompass both physical and emotional aspects. They require time, patience, and often a combination of self-care, support from loved ones, and professional guidance. Each step taken towards healing, no matter how small, is a progression towards reclaiming well-being and peace.

We hope this book was helpful! As we come to the close of this book, we extend our heartfelt thanks to you, our reader, for embarking on this journey with us. Your engagement and willingness to delve into the complexities of the legal world, particularly in the realm of personal injury law, is both appreciated and valued.

We recognize that the topics discussed within these pages are not just legal matters but deeply personal ones that touch the lives of individuals in profound ways. Our aim has been to provide clarity, guidance, and support through the intricacies of legal processes that can often seem daunting and overwhelming.

Remember, the path to justice and recovery, while unique for each individual, does not have to be navigated alone. My experience as a lawyer in this field has equipped me with a wealth of knowledge and insights that I am always ready to share. If you find yourself in need of assistance or guidance or simply wish to discuss your situation further, please do not hesitate to reach out to DiBella Law Offices at www.everycaseispersonal.com or 855-DiBella (855-342-3552).

At DiBella Law Offices, we are here to lend our expertise, support, and counsel whenever you may need it. Your journey is important, and we are committed to helping you every step of the way with the dedication, compassion, and professionalism you deserve.

Thank you once again for reading this book. We wish you strength, hope, and success in all your future endeavors, legal or otherwise. Remember, our door is always open, and our commitment to serving you remains steadfast.

About the Author

Christopher DiBella is the founding partner of DiBella Law Offices, P.C.. Chris brings to the table an impressive and diverse legal background honed over nearly two decades of dedicated legal practice. Licensed in both Massachusetts and New Hampshire, including their respective Federal Courts and the U.S.

Supreme Court, Chris's journey in law is as varied as it is distinguished.

His foray into the legal world was deeply personal. Vivid memories of receiving the harrowing call about his older brother's life-threatening car accident left an indelible mark on him. This incident not only impacted Chris personally but also shaped his understanding of the profound effects such events can have on families. Similarly, stories of his grandfathers, immigrants who faced harsh working conditions in the U.S., and the needless injuries his father endured as a construction laborer further cemented his resolve to pursue justice.

As the first generation in his family to attend college, Chris was propelled onto the path of law by his father. His early introduction to the legal world came in the form of a hefty legal textbook, a gift from his father, symbolizing the hope and expectations of his family. His parents saw the legal profession as a means to effect meaningful change and protect the rights of individuals against injustice.

Chris's career has spanned various facets of law. He began advocating for employees who faced wrongful termination, bringing a voice to those unfairly treated in the workforce. His tenure in the district attorney's office as a prosecutor further broadened his legal acumen, allowing him to serve the community on a broader scale.

Chris's experience in the courtroom is extensive and varied. He has litigated in district court, superior court, appeals court, housing court, and probate court, showcasing his versatility and comprehensive understanding of the legal system. His approach to law is deeply rooted in the belief that legal practice is fundamentally about the people it serves.

At DiBella Law Offices, P.C., Chris leads with a commitment to high-quality legal service, a standard that has earned him numerous awards and accolades. He is honored to be recognized as one of the Top 100 lawyers by The National Trial Lawyers, an invitation-only organization that selects attorneys based on their excellence in and out of the courtroom. This recognition is a testament to his commitment to providing his clients with the highest quality of legal representation.

Additionally, Chris has been distinguished as a “Lawyer of Distinction” by the Lawyers of Distinction organization, a title awarded to attorneys who demonstrate high levels of competence, reputation, and ethical standards. Featured in a New York Times article recognizing the 2021 winners, this accolade further underscores his dedication to his profession and his clients.

In 2014, Christopher DiBella was named one of the "10 Best Under 40" Attorneys for the Commonwealth of Massachusetts by the American Institute of Personal Injury Attorneys. This organization, an impartial third-party attorney rating service, recognizes excellence in the field of personal injury law, extending membership exclusively to those who have reached the pinnacle of their profession.

His prowess in litigation was further acknowledged in 2013 when the American Society of Legal Advocates named him one of the "Top Litigators" in the State of Massachusetts. This invitation-only legal organization comprises less than 1.5% of all licensed lawyers nationwide, emphasizing the select nature of this recognition.

The American Academy of Trial Attorneys, in 2015, included Christopher DiBella in their list of Premier 100 Trial Attorneys. This invitation-only professional organization comprises premier trial attorneys across the nation, recognizing those who have demonstrated exemplary representation of their clients.

Christopher's consistent excellence in the legal field was also recognized through his selection as a Massachusetts Super Lawyer, as featured in Boston Magazine from 2011 through 2023. This honor is bestowed upon attorneys who have demonstrated notable professional achievements and are recognized by their peers for the high standard of service they provide to clients, a distinction limited to no more than 2.5% of the lawyers in the state.

In 2012, The National Trial Lawyers Association named him as one of their Top 40 under 40 - a professional organization composed of the top trial lawyers from each state. Membership in The National Trial Lawyers: Top 40 under 40 is by invitation only and is extended exclusively to those practicing civil plaintiff and/or criminal defense law.

The National Academy of Personal Injury Attorneys, Inc., in 2014, awarded him as one of the Top 10 Attorneys in Massachusetts, a testament to his skill and dedication in the field of personal injury law. This prestigious title is awarded following a rigorous selection process by an independent committee.

Chris DiBella's journey in law is more than a career. It's a lifelong commitment to justice, advocacy, and the belief that everyone deserves fair representation. His diverse experience, deep-rooted passion for justice, and unwavering commitment to his clients continue to be the driving force behind his success and the ethos of DiBella Law Offices, P.C.

Made in United States
North Haven, CT
07 November 2026

21928343R00066